Oracle Fusion: Transforming Hospital Finance

Sushil Kumar

Published by Sushil Kumar, 2025.

ORACLE FUSION:TRANSFORMING HOSPITAL FINANCE

First edition. February 9, 2025.

ISBN: 979-8230061854

Written by Sushil Kumar.

Table of Contents

Introduction

In the fast-paced world of healthcare, financial management can often be the difference between a thriving institution and one struggling to keep its doors open. Imagine a bustling hospital in Dubai, where cutting-edge medical treatments meet traditional values, yet behind the scenes, a financial storm is brewing. This is the story of Al Shifa Hospital, a fictitious yet all-too-real representation of the challenges faced by healthcare providers worldwide. As we delve into the pages of "Oracle Fusion: Transforming Hospital Finance," we embark on a journey that will revolutionize the way we think about healthcare financial management.

The healthcare industry is no stranger to complexity, with its intricate web of patient care, insurance claims, regulatory compliance, and resource allocation. However, in recent years, the financial aspect of running a hospital has become increasingly daunting. With rising costs, evolving payment models, and the constant pressure to improve patient outcomes while maintaining fiscal responsibility, hospital administrators find themselves at a crossroads. It is within this context that our story unfolds, offering a beacon of hope in the form of innovative technology that promises to streamline operations and bring clarity to the murky waters of hospital finance.

"Oracle Fusion: Transforming Hospital Finance" is not just another technical manual or dry account of software implementation. Instead, it presents a compelling narrative that weaves together the human elements of change management with the cutting-edge capabilities of Oracle Fusion Financials. Through the lens of Al Shifa Hospital's journey, readers will gain unprecedented insight into the transformative power of integrated financial systems in a healthcare setting. This book stands out from others in its field by offering a unique blend of storytelling and practical guidance, making complex financial concepts accessible to both seasoned professionals and those new to healthcare finance.

At its core, this book explores several key themes that are critical to understanding the intersection of healthcare and financial management. First and foremost is the concept of digital transformation in healthcare finance. As we follow Al Shifa Hospital's implementation of Oracle Fusion, we witness firsthand how technology can revolutionize traditional financial processes, from general ledger management to patient billing. This theme underscores the importance of embracing technological advancements to stay competitive and efficient in an increasingly digital world.

Another central theme is the importance of data-driven decision-making in healthcare. Throughout the book, we see how Oracle Fusion's robust reporting and analytics capabilities empower hospital leaders to make informed choices based on real-time financial data. This shift from intuition-based to evidence-based management represents a significant paradigm shift in healthcare administration, one that has the potential to improve patient care while optimizing resource allocation.

The book also delves deep into the concept of financial integration within healthcare systems. As we explore the various modules of Oracle Fusion – from Accounts Receivable to Fixed Assets Management – we come to understand how a holistic approach to financial management can break down silos and create a more cohesive operational environment. This integration not only improves efficiency but also enhances transparency and accountability across all levels of the organization.

Compliance and risk management emerge as another crucial theme, particularly relevant in the highly regulated healthcare industry. The book illustrates how advanced financial systems like Oracle Fusion can help hospitals navigate the complex landscape of healthcare regulations, ensuring adherence to legal requirements while streamlining auditing processes. This focus on compliance highlights the dual role of financial systems in not only improving operational efficiency but also in safeguarding the institution against regulatory risks.

Lastly, the book emphasizes the human element of technological change. Through the experiences of Al Shifa Hospital's staff, we explore the challenges and triumphs associated with implementing a new financial system. This theme resonates with anyone who has been part of a large-scale organizational change, offering valuable insights into change management, user training, and the importance of stakeholder buy-in for successful technology adoption.

While "Oracle Fusion: Transforming Hospital Finance" offers valuable insights for a wide range of readers, it is particularly relevant to several key audiences. Hospital administrators, including CEOs, CFOs, and other financial decision-makers, will find the book indispensable as they navigate the complex world of healthcare finance. The practical examples and real-world scenarios presented through Al Shifa Hospital's journey provide a roadmap for leaders looking to modernize their financial operations and drive strategic growth.

Healthcare IT professionals will also find immense value in this book. As the bridge between technology and healthcare operations, these individuals play a crucial role in implementing and maintaining financial systems. The detailed exploration of Oracle Fusion's capabilities, integration challenges, and customization options offers a wealth of knowledge that can be applied to real-world implementations.

Finance professionals working in healthcare settings, from accountants to financial analysts, will discover new ways to leverage technology to enhance their work. The book's in-depth coverage of various financial modules and processes provides practical knowledge that can be immediately applied to improve financial reporting, budgeting, and forecasting activities.

Additionally, healthcare consultants and advisors will find this book to be an excellent resource for understanding the latest trends in healthcare financial management. The comprehensive analysis of Oracle Fusion's impact on hospital operations offers valuable insights that can inform consulting strategies and recommendations for healthcare clients.

Readers of "Oracle Fusion: Transforming Hospital Finance" will gain a multitude of benefits that extend far beyond a simple understanding of software functionality. First and foremost, they will develop a comprehensive understanding of how integrated financial systems can transform healthcare operations. This knowledge is invaluable in an era where digital transformation is no longer optional but essential for survival and growth in the healthcare industry.

The book also provides readers with a framework for evaluating and implementing large-scale financial systems in healthcare settings. By following Al Shifa Hospital's journey from initial assessment to full implementation and beyond, readers will gain insights into best practices, potential pitfalls, and critical success factors for similar projects in their own organizations. This practical knowledge can save institutions significant time and resources when undertaking their own digital transformation initiatives.

Furthermore, readers will develop a deeper appreciation for the strategic role of finance in healthcare delivery. The book illustrates how financial systems are not just back-office tools but strategic assets that can drive improvements in patient care, operational efficiency, and overall organizational performance. This perspective can help readers elevate the role of finance within their own organizations, positioning it as a key driver of strategic decision-making.

The book also offers valuable insights into change management and organizational culture in healthcare settings. By exploring the human aspects of technology implementation, readers will gain strategies for managing resistance to change, fostering user adoption, and building a culture of continuous improvement. These soft skills are often the difference between success and failure in large-scale technology projects.

Moreover, readers will enhance their understanding of healthcare compliance and risk management. The book's exploration of how Oracle Fusion supports regulatory adherence and simplifies auditing processes provides valuable knowledge for navigating the complex regulatory landscape of the healthcare industry. This understanding can help readers build more robust compliance frameworks within their own organizations.

Lastly, the book provides a window into the future of healthcare finance. By showcasing the advanced capabilities of Oracle Fusion, including its powerful analytics and reporting tools, the book helps readers envision the possibilities for data-driven decision-making in healthcare. This forward-looking perspective can inspire innovation and strategic thinking, positioning readers to lead their organizations into the future of healthcare finance.

As we embark on this journey through the pages of "Oracle Fusion: Transforming Hospital Finance," we invite you to imagine the possibilities for your own healthcare organization. Whether you're grappling with outdated financial systems, struggling to meet regulatory requirements, or simply seeking ways to optimize your financial operations, this book offers a roadmap to success. Through the trials and triumphs of Al Shifa Hospital, you'll discover not just the technical aspects of implementing a world-class financial system, but also the human story of transformation and growth.

The healthcare industry stands at a crossroads, faced with unprecedented challenges and extraordinary opportunities. As we explore the power of Oracle Fusion to revolutionize hospital finance, we'll uncover insights that extend far beyond software implementation. We'll delve into the heart of what it means to deliver high-quality healthcare in a financially sustainable manner, exploring how technology can be a catalyst for positive change across entire organizations.

Prepare to be inspired by the potential for innovation in healthcare finance. Expect to be challenged to think differently about the role of financial systems in delivering patient care. And most importantly, get ready to envision a future where financial clarity and operational excellence go hand in hand, driving better outcomes for patients, staff, and communities alike.

As we turn the page to Chapter 1, we step into the world of Al Shifa Hospital, where a financial dilemma is about to spark a transformation that will resonate with healthcare providers around the globe. The journey ahead is filled with valuable lessons, practical insights, and transformative ideas that have the power to reshape the landscape of healthcare finance. So, let's begin this exploration of how Oracle Fusion is not just changing systems, but transforming the very essence of hospital financial management for the better.

Chapter 1 - Setting the Stage: Al Shifa Hospital's Financial Dilemma

A Beacon of Hope in Dubai's Healthcare Landscape

As the sun rose over the gleaming skyline of Dubai, casting a golden glow on the modern architecture that defined the city's landscape, the imposing structure of Al Shifa Hospital stood as a testament to the emirate's commitment to world-class healthcare. Established just five years ago, Al Shifa had quickly become a beacon of hope for patients seeking cutting-edge medical treatments in the Middle East.

The hospital's state-of-the-art facilities, coupled with its team of internationally renowned medical professionals, had earned it a reputation as one of the region's premier healthcare institutions. From its advanced oncology center to its pioneering robotic surgery unit, Al Shifa Hospital embodied Dubai's vision of becoming a global hub for medical tourism and excellence.

Meet the Visionaries: Dr. Aisha Al Mansoori and Yusuf Khalil

At the helm of this healthcare marvel stood two individuals whose passion for medical innovation was matched only by their commitment to operational excellence. Dr. Aisha Al Mansoori, the hospital's charismatic CEO, was a force to be reckoned with in the medical community. With her background in neurosurgery and a Ph.D. in healthcare management from Harvard, Dr. Al Mansoori brought a unique blend of clinical expertise and business acumen to her role.

Her piercing brown eyes, often alight with enthusiasm, belied the weight of responsibility she carried on her shoulders. At 45, Dr. Al Mansoori had already achieved more than most do in a lifetime, but she knew that the true measure of her success would be Al Shifa's ability to sustainably provide world-class healthcare to the diverse population of Dubai and beyond.

Working alongside Dr. Al Mansoori was Yusuf Khalil, the hospital's Chief Financial Officer. A seasoned financial expert with over two decades of experience in healthcare finance, Yusuf's calm demeanor and analytical mind provided the perfect counterbalance to Dr. Al Mansoori's visionary zeal. At 50, with graying temples and a penchant for crisp white shirts, Yusuf exuded an air of quiet confidence that reassured both staff and stakeholders alike.

Together, this dynamic duo had steered Al Shifa through its initial years of operation, overcoming countless challenges and celebrating numerous victories. However, as they sat in Dr. Al Mansoori's spacious office overlooking the Dubai skyline, both knew that they were facing their greatest challenge yet.

The Gathering Storm: Al Shifa's Financial Challenges

The morning sun streamed through the floor-to-ceiling windows, illuminating the concerned expressions on both their faces as they pored over the latest financial reports. Yusuf's usually steady hand trembled slightly as he pointed to a particularly troubling line item.

"Dr. Al Mansoori, I'm afraid our accounts receivable have ballooned to an unprecedented level," Yusuf began, his voice tinged with worry. "We're currently sitting on over 200 million dirhams in unpaid bills, with nearly 30% of those being over 90 days past due."

Dr. Al Mansoori leaned back in her chair, her brow furrowed in concentration. "That's certainly alarming, Yusuf. What's causing this spike?"

Yusuf sighed, flipping through several pages of the report. "There are multiple factors at play here. Firstly, we're seeing delays in reimbursements from insurance companies. Many of our innovative treatments, particularly in oncology and neurology, are facing scrutiny and prolonged approval processes."

He continued, "Additionally, our international patient base, which accounts for a significant portion of our revenue, has been growing rapidly. While this is excellent news for our reputation, it's also leading to complications in billing and collection across different countries and healthcare systems."

Dr. Al Mansoori nodded thoughtfully. "I see. And how is this affecting our cash flow?"

"That's where things get even more concerning," Yusuf replied, turning to another page in the report. "Our days cash on hand has dropped to just 45 days. For a hospital of our size and complexity, we should be aiming for at least 150 days. This severe cash crunch is hampering our ability to invest in new equipment, expand our services, and even meet our day-to-day operational expenses."

The Ripple Effect: Operational Challenges

As the gravity of the situation sank in, Dr. Al Mansoori stood up and walked to the window, her reflection superimposed on the bustling city below. She turned back to Yusuf, her expression a mix of concern and determination.

"Yusuf, help me understand how this financial strain is impacting our operations on the ground."

Yusuf pulled out another set of documents from his briefcase. "The effects are far-reaching, I'm afraid. Our procurement department is struggling to maintain adequate inventory levels of critical medical supplies. We've had to delay payments to several key vendors, which is straining our relationships and, in some cases, leading to supply shortages."

He paused, his voice lowering. "Just last week, Dr. Fatima from Cardiology reported that a critical procedure had to be postponed because we didn't have the necessary specialized equipment in stock. The patient had to be referred to another hospital."

Dr. Al Mansoori's eyes widened at this news. "That's unacceptable. Our patients' care cannot be compromised due to financial constraints. What else?"

Yusuf continued, "Our plans for expanding the pediatric wing have been put on hold indefinitely. The construction company is unwilling to proceed without a substantial down payment, which we simply can't afford right now."

He flipped to another page. "Moreover, our staff morale is taking a hit. We've had to freeze hiring for several critical positions, leading to increased workloads for our existing staff. There are also whispers of potential delays in salary payments if our cash flow situation doesn't improve soon."

The Root Causes: Digging Deeper

Dr. Al Mansoori returned to her seat, her mind racing as she processed the information. "Yusuf, we need to get to the root of this problem. Beyond the delayed reimbursements and international billing complexities, what other factors are contributing to this financial crisis?"

Yusuf leaned forward, his fingers steepled in thought. "There are several systemic issues that we've identified. Our current financial management system is outdated and ill-equipped to handle the complexity of our operations. We're relying heavily on manual processes, which are not only time-consuming but also prone to errors."

He elaborated, "For instance, our billing department is struggling to keep up with the volume of claims, leading to delays in submission and a higher rate of rejections due to errors. Our accounts payable process is equally cumbersome, making it difficult to optimize our cash outflows or take advantage of early payment discounts from suppliers."

Dr. Al Mansoori nodded, encouraging him to continue.

"Furthermore," Yusuf went on, "our financial reporting capabilities are limited. We lack real-time visibility into our financial position, making it challenging to make informed decisions quickly. Our budgeting and forecasting processes are also largely manual, reducing their accuracy and making it difficult to adapt to changing circumstances."

He paused, taking a deep breath before addressing perhaps the most critical issue. "Lastly, and this is perhaps the most concerning, our current system lacks robust internal controls. This not only increases our risk of fraud but also makes our audit processes incredibly time-consuming and costly."

The Compliance Conundrum

Dr. Al Mansoori's expression grew even more serious at the mention of internal controls. "Yusuf, given the regulatory landscape in healthcare, how exposed are we from a compliance standpoint?"

Yusuf's face tightened. "I'm glad you asked, Dr. Al Mansoori. Our current financial management system is making it increasingly difficult to meet the stringent regulatory requirements we face."

He pulled out a thick binder labeled 'Regulatory Compliance' from his briefcase. "As you know, we're subject to oversight from multiple bodies – the Dubai Health Authority, the UAE Ministry of Health and Prevention, and for our international accreditations, organizations like Joint Commission International."

Flipping through the binder, he continued, "Our manual processes and lack of robust audit trails make it challenging to demonstrate compliance with financial regulations. We're spending an inordinate amount of time and resources on preparing for audits, and even then, we're at risk of non-compliance due to potential oversights or errors."

Dr. Al Mansoori leaned forward, her concern evident. "What specific areas are most at risk?"

Yusuf sighed, "Several critical areas, I'm afraid. Our revenue cycle management, particularly in terms of accurate coding and billing, is one major concern. We're at risk of inadvertently submitting incorrect claims, which could lead to accusations of fraud or abuse."

He flipped to another section of the binder. "Additionally, our fixed asset management is suboptimal. We're struggling to maintain accurate records of our medical equipment, their depreciation, and maintenance schedules. This not only affects our financial statements but also poses potential patient safety risks if equipment maintenance is not properly tracked."

"Perhaps most alarmingly," Yusuf continued, his voice lowering, "our current system makes it difficult to implement and demonstrate the kind of financial controls required by regulations like the Sarbanes-Oxley Act. While we're not directly subject to SOX, many of our international partners and potential investors expect similar levels of financial governance."

Dr. Al Mansoori sat back, the weight of the situation fully sinking in. "This is indeed serious, Yusuf. It seems our financial challenges are not just impacting our operations but potentially putting our very license to operate at risk."

The Human Cost: Beyond Numbers

As the gravity of the situation settled in the room, Dr. Al Mansoori's gaze drifted to a framed photo on her desk. It showed her shaking hands with a smiling young girl, bald from chemotherapy but with eyes full of hope. The image served as a poignant reminder of why they were all here – to heal, to care, to make a difference.

"Yusuf," she began, her voice soft but resolute, "behind every number in these reports, there's a patient, a family, a life hanging in the balance. Our financial health directly impacts our ability to fulfill our mission of providing world-class healthcare to those who need it most."

Yusuf nodded solemnly, understanding the weight of her words.

Dr. Al Mansoori continued, "Just last week, I met with the family of Ahmed, a 7-year-old boy who needs a specialized heart surgery.

We have the expertise to perform this life-saving procedure, but if our financial situation doesn't improve, we might have to start turning away complex cases like Ahmed's. The thought of that is unbearable."

She stood up and walked to a wall adorned with the hospital's awards and accolades. "We've built something remarkable here, Yusuf. Al Shifa isn't just a hospital; it's a symbol of hope for countless patients across the region. We cannot let financial constraints dim that hope."

Yusuf rose to join her, his resolve strengthening. "You're absolutely right, Dr. Al Mansoori. We owe it to Ahmed, to all our patients, and to our dedicated staff to find a solution. But I must admit, the challenges we face are complex and multifaceted. We need a comprehensive approach that addresses not just our immediate cash flow issues but also the underlying systemic problems in our financial management."

The Search for Solutions

Dr. Al Mansoori turned to face Yusuf, her eyes glinting with determination. "You're right, Yusuf. We need a solution that's as sophisticated and forward-thinking as the medical care we provide. What options have you explored so far?"

Yusuf pulled out a tablet from his briefcase and pulled up a presentation. "I've been researching various financial management solutions that could address our complex needs. Given the scale and nature of our operations, we need a system that can handle everything from basic accounting to advanced financial analytics and reporting."

He swiped through several slides, explaining, "I've looked into several options, from upgrading our current system to implementing a completely new ERP solution. However, given our unique position as a cutting-edge hospital with international operations, most off-the-shelf solutions fall short in one area or another."

Dr. Al Mansoori nodded, encouraging him to continue.

"There is, however, one solution that stands out," Yusuf said, his voice taking on a hint of excitement for the first time that morning.

"Oracle Fusion Financials. It's a cloud-based financial management system that seems tailor-made for an organization of our complexity and ambition."

He pulled up a detailed slide about Oracle Fusion. "It offers a comprehensive suite of financial applications – from general ledger and accounts receivable to fixed assets and cash management. But what really sets it apart is its ability to handle multi-currency, multi-entity operations, which is crucial for our international patient base."

Dr. Al Mansoori leaned in, her interest piqued. "That does sound promising. But implementing a new financial system is a massive undertaking. How disruptive would this be to our ongoing operations?"

Yusuf nodded, acknowledging her concern. "You're right, it would be a significant project. However, being cloud-based, Oracle Fusion offers faster implementation times compared to traditional on-premise solutions. Moreover, it's designed to integrate seamlessly with other healthcare systems, which could actually streamline many of our processes in the long run."

He paused, then added, "But perhaps most importantly, it could provide us with the real-time financial visibility and robust compliance features we desperately need. The advanced analytics and reporting capabilities could transform how we make financial decisions."

The Road Ahead: A Glimpse of Hope

Dr. Al Mansoori walked back to her desk, her mind processing the information. She picked up the photo of the young cancer patient, studying it intently. After a moment of reflection, she looked up at Yusuf, her decision made.

"Yusuf, I believe we've found our path forward. Oracle Fusion sounds like it could be the comprehensive solution we need. But before we commit, I want to be certain. Can you arrange a detailed presentation from Oracle? I want to see exactly how this system could address our specific challenges."

Yusuf nodded eagerly, already pulling out his phone. "Absolutely, Dr. Al Mansoori. I'll set it up right away. I believe they have a team here in Dubai that specializes in healthcare implementations."

Dr. Al Mansoori smiled, feeling a renewed sense of hope. "Excellent. And Yusuf, let's keep this between us for now. I don't want to raise expectations until we're sure this is the right move. But do start putting together a team – we'll need our best minds from finance, IT, and operations if we decide to move forward with this."

Yusuf nodded in agreement, already making mental notes of who to involve.

"One more thing," Dr. Al Mansoori added, her voice taking on a note of determination. "I want you to prepare a presentation for the board. They need to understand the full scope of our financial challenges and why a solution like Oracle Fusion is necessary. We'll need their full support for a project of this magnitude."

Yusuf straightened, recognizing the challenge ahead. "Understood, Dr. Al Mansoori. I'll have a comprehensive presentation ready for the next board meeting."

As Yusuf gathered his documents and prepared to leave, Dr. Al Mansoori called out, "Yusuf, thank you for bringing this to my attention and for your diligence in seeking solutions. Al Shifa's mission is too important to let financial constraints hold us back. Together, we'll find a way to not just overcome this challenge but to emerge stronger and better equipped to serve our patients."

Yusuf paused at the door, turning back with a smile. "Thank you, Dr. Al Mansoori. Your leadership and vision are what make Al Shifa special. I'm confident that with the right tools and your guidance, we'll not only weather this storm but set new standards for financial management in healthcare."

As the door closed behind Yusuf, Dr. Al Mansoori turned to gaze out at the Dubai skyline once more. The city's iconic buildings stood as a testament to ambition, innovation, and the ability to overcome seemingly insurmountable challenges. She knew that Al Shifa Hospital, with its dedicated team and potentially transformative new financial system, was poised to write its own success story.

The path ahead would not be easy. Implementing a new financial management system would require careful planning, seamless execution, and unwavering commitment from every member of the Al Shifa family. But as Dr. Al Mansoori looked at the photo of the smiling young patient on her desk, she knew that every effort, every challenge overcome, would be worth it.

For in the end, this wasn't just about balancing books or streamlining processes. It was about ensuring that Al Shifa Hospital could continue to be a beacon of hope, healing, and healthcare excellence for generations to come. With renewed determination, Dr. Al Mansoori picked up her phone to schedule an emergency board meeting. The journey to transform Al Shifa's financial future was about to begin.

Chapter 2 - The Oracle Fusion Solution: An Overview

Introduction to Oracle Fusion Financials

As Al Shifa Hospital grapples with its financial challenges, a beacon of hope emerges in the form of Oracle Fusion Financials. This powerful, cloud-based solution promises to revolutionize the hospital's financial management processes, offering a comprehensive suite of tools designed to streamline operations, enhance decision-making, and drive financial success.

Oracle Fusion Financials is not just another software package; it's a transformative platform that combines cutting-edge technology with industry best practices to deliver a holistic approach to financial management. For Al Shifa Hospital, this solution represents an opportunity to overcome its current financial hurdles and pave the way for a more prosperous future.

The Evolution of Financial Management Systems

To fully appreciate the capabilities of Oracle Fusion Financials, it's essential to understand the evolution of financial management systems in healthcare. Historically, hospitals relied on a patchwork of disparate systems and manual processes to manage their finances. This approach often led to inefficiencies, data inconsistencies, and a lack of real-time visibility into financial performance.

As technology advanced, standalone financial management software emerged, offering improved functionality but still lacking the integration and scalability needed to meet the complex needs of modern healthcare organizations. Oracle Fusion Financials represents the next generation of financial management solutions, built from the ground up to address these limitations and provide a unified, flexible platform for healthcare finance.

Key Components of Oracle Fusion Financials

Oracle Fusion Financials is comprised of several interconnected modules, each designed to address specific aspects of financial management. While subsequent chapters will delve into these modules in greater detail, here's a high-level overview of the key components:

1. General Ledger
2. Accounts Receivable
3. Accounts Payable
4. Fixed Assets
5. Cash Management
6. Budgeting and Forecasting
7. Financial Reporting and Analytics

These modules work in concert to provide a comprehensive financial management solution, enabling Al Shifa Hospital to streamline its processes, improve accuracy, and gain deeper insights into its financial performance.

Cloud-Based Architecture: A Game-Changer for Healthcare Finance

One of the most significant advantages of Oracle Fusion Financials is its cloud-based architecture. This approach offers numerous benefits for healthcare organizations like Al Shifa Hospital:

Scalability and Flexibility

Cloud-based solutions allow hospitals to easily scale their financial management capabilities as they grow or face changing market conditions. Al Shifa Hospital can add new users, modules, or functionalities without the need for extensive hardware upgrades or IT infrastructure investments.

Reduced IT Burden

By leveraging Oracle's cloud infrastructure, Al Shifa Hospital can significantly reduce its IT overhead. Oracle manages the hardware, software updates, and security patches, allowing the hospital's IT team to focus on more strategic initiatives.

Anytime, Anywhere Access

Cloud-based systems enable authorized users to access financial information and perform tasks from any device with an internet connection. This flexibility is particularly valuable in a hospital setting, where decision-makers may need to access critical financial data outside of regular office hours or locations.

Enhanced Security and Compliance

Oracle Fusion Financials incorporates robust security measures and compliance features, helping Al Shifa Hospital protect sensitive financial data and adhere to regulatory requirements. Regular updates ensure that the system remains current with evolving security standards and compliance regulations.

Real-Time Financial Visibility and Insights

One of the most compelling features of Oracle Fusion Financials is its ability to provide real-time visibility into the hospital's financial performance. This capability addresses one of Al Shifa Hospital's primary pain points: the lack of timely, accurate financial information for decision-making.

Dashboards and Analytics

Oracle Fusion Financials offers customizable dashboards that present key financial metrics and performance indicators in easy-to-understand visual formats. Hospital executives and finance team members can quickly assess the organization's financial health, identify trends, and spot potential issues before they escalate.

Ad-Hoc Reporting

The solution's powerful reporting tools allow users to create custom reports on demand, without relying on IT support. This flexibility enables Al Shifa Hospital's finance team to respond quickly to information requests from stakeholders and make data-driven decisions with confidence.

Predictive Analytics

Oracle Fusion Financials incorporates advanced analytics capabilities, including predictive modeling. These tools can help Al Shifa Hospital forecast future financial performance, anticipate cash flow challenges, and identify opportunities for cost savings or revenue growth.

Streamlined Financial Processes

Efficiency is critical in healthcare finance, and Oracle Fusion Financials offers numerous features designed to streamline and automate key financial processes:

Automated Journal Entries

The system can automatically generate and post routine journal entries, reducing the risk of errors and freeing up finance staff to focus on more strategic tasks.

Intelligent Document Recognition

Oracle Fusion Financials uses advanced OCR (Optical Character Recognition) technology to automatically extract data from invoices and other financial documents, significantly reducing manual data entry and improving accuracy.

Workflow Automation

Built-in workflow tools allow Al Shifa Hospital to automate approval processes, ensuring that financial transactions are reviewed and authorized by the appropriate personnel in a timely manner.

Reconciliation Management

The solution includes tools to streamline the account reconciliation process, reducing the time and effort required to close the books each period.

Enhanced Financial Control and Risk Management

For a healthcare organization like Al Shifa Hospital, maintaining strong financial controls and managing risk is paramount. Oracle Fusion Financials offers several features to support these objectives:

Segregation of Duties

The system allows for granular control over user access and permissions, ensuring that sensitive financial tasks are appropriately segregated to prevent fraud and errors.

Audit Trails

Comprehensive audit trails provide a detailed record of all financial transactions and system changes, supporting internal control efforts and simplifying external audits.

Risk Management Tools

Oracle Fusion Financials includes built-in risk management capabilities, helping Al Shifa Hospital identify and mitigate financial risks proactively.

Integration Capabilities

While Oracle Fusion Financials offers a comprehensive suite of financial management tools, it's also designed to integrate seamlessly with other systems and data sources. This integration capability is crucial for Al Shifa Hospital, which likely relies on various specialized healthcare systems.

EHR Integration

Oracle Fusion Financials can integrate with Electronic Health Record (EHR) systems, enabling a smooth flow of financial data related to patient care and billing.

Supply Chain Management

The solution can connect with supply chain management systems, providing a holistic view of procurement costs and inventory levels.

Human Resources and Payroll

Integration with HR and payroll systems ensures accurate tracking of labor costs and streamlines the management of employee-related expenses.

Mobile Capabilities

In today's fast-paced healthcare environment, the ability to access financial information and perform tasks on the go is invaluable. Oracle Fusion Financials offers robust mobile capabilities:

Mobile Approvals

Managers can review and approve financial transactions, such as purchase orders or expense reports, from their mobile devices, preventing bottlenecks in the approval process.

Mobile Analytics

Key financial metrics and reports can be accessed via mobile devices, allowing decision-makers to stay informed even when they're away from their desks.

Mobile Expense Management

Staff members can easily submit expense reports and capture receipts using their smartphones, streamlining the reimbursement process.

Artificial Intelligence and Machine Learning

Oracle Fusion Financials leverages cutting-edge AI and machine learning technologies to enhance its capabilities and provide even greater value to organizations like Al Shifa Hospital:

Intelligent Process Automation

AI-powered algorithms can learn from historical data and user behavior to automate routine tasks and suggest process improvements.

Anomaly Detection

Machine learning models can identify unusual patterns or transactions in financial data, alerting staff to potential errors or fraudulent activities.

Predictive Cash Flow Management

AI-driven predictive models can help Al Shifa Hospital forecast cash flow more accurately, taking into account a wide range of variables and historical trends.

Continuous Innovation and Updates

One of the significant advantages of Oracle Fusion Financials' cloud-based model is the regular release of new features and improvements. This ensures that Al Shifa Hospital always has access to the latest financial management capabilities without the need for disruptive upgrades:

Quarterly Updates

Oracle provides quarterly updates to the system, introducing new features, enhancements, and bug fixes.

User-Driven Innovation

Oracle actively solicits feedback from its user community, incorporating customer suggestions into its product roadmap.

Industry-Specific Enhancements

As a leader in healthcare technology, Oracle regularly introduces new features specifically designed to address the unique needs of healthcare organizations like Al Shifa Hospital.

Cost-Effectiveness and ROI

While the capabilities of Oracle Fusion Financials are impressive, Al Shifa Hospital's leadership team is undoubtedly concerned about the cost and potential return on investment. It's important to note that the cloud-based model offers several financial advantages:

Reduced Capital Expenditure

As a cloud solution, Oracle Fusion Financials eliminates the need for significant upfront investments in hardware and infrastructure.

Predictable Operating Expenses

The subscription-based pricing model allows for more predictable budgeting of IT expenses.

Rapid Time to Value

Cloud deployment typically allows for faster implementation and a quicker realization of benefits compared to traditional on-premises solutions.

Total Cost of Ownership

When considering factors such as reduced IT staffing needs, eliminated hardware costs, and improved efficiency, many organizations find that Oracle Fusion Financials offers a lower total cost of ownership compared to legacy systems or competing solutions.

User Experience and Adoption

The success of any financial management system depends heavily on user adoption. Oracle Fusion Financials is designed with the end-user in mind, offering an intuitive interface and features that promote rapid adoption:

Role-Based User Interface

The system presents a personalized experience based on each user's role and responsibilities, streamlining navigation and improving efficiency.

Natural Language Processing

Users can interact with the system using natural language queries, making it easier to find information and perform tasks without extensive training.

Contextual Help and Guidance

Built-in help features and guided workflows assist users in completing complex tasks, reducing the learning curve and improving productivity.

Sustainability and Corporate Social Responsibility

As healthcare organizations increasingly focus on sustainability and corporate social responsibility, Oracle Fusion Financials offers features to support these initiatives:

Environmental Impact Tracking

The system can help Al Shifa Hospital track and report on its environmental impact, including energy consumption and waste management.

Supplier Sustainability Monitoring

Oracle Fusion Financials can assist in monitoring and reporting on the sustainability practices of suppliers, supporting responsible procurement efforts.

CSR Reporting

Built-in reporting tools can help Al Shifa Hospital generate comprehensive corporate social responsibility reports, demonstrating its commitment to community health and well-being.

Conclusion: A Transformative Solution for Al Shifa Hospital

Oracle Fusion Financials represents a transformative opportunity for Al Shifa Hospital to overcome its current financial challenges and position itself for long-term success. By providing a comprehensive, integrated, and technologically advanced financial management platform, this solution addresses many of the pain points facing modern healthcare organizations.

From real-time financial visibility and streamlined processes to enhanced control and risk management, Oracle Fusion Financials offers a wide range of capabilities that can drive significant improvements in Al Shifa Hospital's financial operations. The cloud-based architecture ensures scalability, security, and continuous innovation, while the user-friendly interface and mobile capabilities promote widespread adoption and productivity.

As Al Shifa Hospital's leadership team considers this solution, they can be confident that Oracle Fusion Financials has the potential to not only solve their immediate financial dilemmas but also to provide a solid foundation for future growth and success. The journey ahead will require careful planning, change management, and a commitment to leveraging the full potential of this powerful platform. However, with Oracle Fusion Financials as their financial management cornerstone, Al Shifa Hospital is well-positioned to transform its financial operations and focus on its core mission of providing exceptional patient care.

Chapter 3 - Project Kickoff: Defining Objectives and Scope

Setting the Stage for Transformation

As the morning sun cast its golden rays over the gleaming façade of Al Shifa Hospital, an air of anticipation filled the boardroom on the top floor. Today marked the beginning of a journey that would transform the financial landscape of this prestigious Dubai healthcare institution. The hospital's leadership team, led by CEO Dr. Amira Khalid and CFO Rashid Al-Mansoori, sat around the polished mahogany table, their expressions a mix of excitement and determination.

Across from them, a team of Oracle consultants, led by the seasoned implementation expert, Sarah Thompson, arranged their laptops and presentation materials. The tension in the room was palpable as both parties recognized the magnitude of the task ahead: implementing Oracle Fusion Financials to revolutionize Al Shifa Hospital's financial operations.

Dr. Khalid cleared her throat, her voice steady as she addressed the room. "Ladies and gentlemen, today we embark on a crucial mission to secure the financial future of Al Shifa Hospital. Our partnership with Oracle represents not just a system upgrade, but a complete reimagining of how we manage our finances. Let's begin by clearly defining our objectives and scope for this project."

Establishing Clear Objectives

Sarah Thompson nodded in agreement and stood up, her posture exuding confidence. "Thank you, Dr. Khalid. You're absolutely right. The first step in any successful implementation is to establish clear, measurable objectives. Let's start by discussing what Al Shifa Hospital hopes to achieve through this Oracle Fusion implementation."

Rashid Al-Mansoori, the CFO, leaned forward, his brow furrowed in concentration. "Our primary goal is to streamline our financial processes and gain real-time visibility into our financial health. We need to improve our cash flow management, reduce billing errors, and enhance our reporting capabilities."

Dr. Khalid chimed in, "Additionally, we want to ensure compliance with international healthcare financial regulations and improve our decision-making process through data-driven insights."

As the discussion progressed, the Oracle team diligently noted down the key objectives:

1. Streamline financial processes
2. Achieve real-time financial visibility
3. Improve cash flow management
4. Reduce billing errors
5. Enhance reporting capabilities
6. Ensure regulatory compliance
7. Enable data-driven decision-making

Sarah Thompson nodded approvingly. "These are excellent objectives, and I'm confident that Oracle Fusion Financials can help you achieve them. Now, let's break these down into more specific, measurable goals."

Defining Measurable Goals

The room buzzed with activity as the team worked together to transform the broad objectives into concrete, quantifiable goals. After intense discussion and negotiation, they arrived at the following:

1. Reduce month-end close process from 15 days to 5 days within six months of go-live
2. Decrease Days Sales Outstanding (DSO) by 20% within the

first year

3. Achieve 99% accuracy in patient billing within three months of implementation
4. Generate comprehensive financial reports within 24 hours of request, compared to the current 5-7 day turnaround
5. Ensure 100% compliance with IFRS (International Financial Reporting Standards) and local UAE healthcare financial regulations
6. Reduce manual data entry by 80% through automation and integration
7. Provide real-time access to key financial metrics for executive decision-making

Dr. Khalid nodded satisfactorily. "These goals are ambitious but achievable. They will significantly improve our financial operations and position us for future growth."

Defining Project Scope

With the objectives and goals clearly established, the team turned their attention to defining the project scope. Sarah Thompson took the lead, her voice clear and authoritative.

"Now that we have our goals in place, let's outline what will be included in this implementation project, as well as what will be excluded. This will help us manage expectations and resources effectively."

The discussion that followed was both lively and focused, with both the hospital team and Oracle consultants contributing their expertise. After careful consideration, they agreed on the following scope:

In Scope:

1. Implementation of Oracle Fusion Financials modules:

o General Ledger

o Accounts Receivable

o Accounts Payable

o Fixed Assets

o Cash Management

2. Integration with existing Hospital Information System (HIS) for seamless data flow

3. Data migration from legacy systems to Oracle Fusion

4. Customization of reports to meet Al Shifa Hospital's specific requirements

5. User training for finance staff and key stakeholders

6. Post-implementation support for three months

Out of Scope:

1. Implementation of non-financial Oracle Fusion modules (e.g., Human Capital Management, Supply Chain Management)
2. Hardware upgrades or network infrastructure changes
3. Historical data migration beyond the agreed-upon timeframe (last 3 years)
4. Customization of core Oracle Fusion functionality

Rashid Al-Mansoori, the CFO, raised a concern. "I understand the need to limit scope, but I'm worried about the exclusion of Supply Chain Management. Our procurement process is closely tied to our financials."

Sarah Thompson nodded understandingly. "That's a valid concern, Rashid. While we won't be implementing the full Supply Chain Management module in this phase, we can ensure that the financial aspects of procurement are covered within the Accounts Payable module. We can also discuss a phased approach to implementing additional modules in the future."

This compromise seemed to satisfy the CFO, and the team moved on to discuss the project timeline and resources.

Project Timeline and Milestones

With the scope defined, the next crucial step was to establish a realistic timeline for the implementation. Sarah Thompson pulled up a Gantt chart on the projector, outlining the proposed project phases and milestones.

"Based on our experience with similar implementations and the scope we've defined, we're looking at a total project duration of approximately 12 months," Sarah explained. "This timeline allows for thorough planning, execution, and testing, while also accounting for the complexities of integrating with your existing systems."

The proposed timeline was broken down into the following phases and milestones:

1. Project Initiation and Planning (1 month)

○ Milestone: Project Charter Signed

2. Business Process Analysis and Design (2 months)

○ Milestone: Business Requirements Document Approved

3. System Configuration and Customization (3 months)

  ○ Milestone: System Configuration Complete

4. Data Migration (2 months)

  ○ Milestone: Data Migration Tested and Validated

5. Integration and Testing (2 months)

  ○ Milestone: User Acceptance Testing Completed

6. User Training (1 month)

  ○ Milestone: Training Programs Completed

7. Go-Live Preparation (2 weeks)

  ○ Milestone: Go-Live Readiness Assessment Passed

8. Go-Live and Stabilization (2 weeks)

  ○ Milestone: System Go-Live

9. Post-Implementation Support (3 months)

  ○ Milestone: Project Closure and Handover

Dr. Khalid studied the timeline carefully. "This seems comprehensive, but I'm concerned about the impact on our day-to-day operations, especially during the go-live phase."

Sarah reassured her, "We understand your concerns, Dr. Khalid. Our approach includes strategies to minimize disruption, such as parallel running of systems and phased cutover. We'll work closely with your team to ensure business continuity throughout the implementation."

Resource Allocation and Team Structure

With the timeline established, the discussion turned to the crucial topic of resource allocation. Both Al Shifa Hospital and Oracle needed to commit significant resources to ensure the project's success.

Sarah Thompson outlined the proposed team structure:

1. Executive Steering Committee

○ Al Shifa Hospital: CEO, CFO, CIO

○ Oracle: Senior Account Executive, Project Director

2. Project Management Office (PMO)

○ Al Shifa Hospital: Project Manager, Change Management Lead

○ Oracle: Senior Project Manager, Quality Assurance Lead

3. Functional Team

○ Al Shifa Hospital: Finance Subject Matter Experts (SMEs) for each module

○ Oracle: Functional Consultants for each module

4. Technical Team

○ Al Shifa Hospital: IT Lead, Database Administrator, Network Administrator

○ Oracle: Technical Architect, Integration Specialist, Database Specialist

5. Change Management and Training Team

○ Al Shifa Hospital: HR Representative, Department Heads

○ Oracle: Change Management Consultant, Training Specialist

Rashid Al-Mansoori, the CFO, looked concerned. "This is a significant commitment of resources on our part. How can we ensure that our staff can balance their day-to-day responsibilities with the project demands?"

Sarah nodded, acknowledging the valid concern. "It's a challenge we often face in implementations. We recommend a few strategies:

1. Temporary staff augmentation for routine tasks
2. Clear communication of project importance and adjusted performance expectations
3. Flexible working arrangements, including some after-hours project work
4. Regular workload reviews and adjustments as needed

Remember, this investment of time and resources will pay off in improved efficiency and effectiveness once the system is implemented."

Risk Assessment and Mitigation Strategies

As the meeting progressed, the team turned their attention to identifying potential risks and developing mitigation strategies. Sarah Thompson facilitated a brainstorming session, encouraging both the hospital team and Oracle consultants to voice their concerns openly.

After a thorough discussion, they identified the following key risks:

1. Resistance to change from hospital staff
2. Data migration errors or inconsistencies
3. Integration challenges with existing systems
4. Scope creep leading to project delays and cost overruns
5. Inadequate user adoption post-implementation
6. Regulatory compliance issues
7. System performance concerns

For each identified risk, the team developed mitigation strategies:

1. Resistance to change:

○ Implement a robust change management program

○ Engage staff early and often through regular communications

○ Highlight benefits of the new system for individual roles

2. Data migration issues:

○ Conduct thorough data cleansing before migration

○ Perform multiple rounds of data validation

○ Plan for manual data verification for critical financial information

3. Integration challenges:

○ Conduct detailed analysis of existing systems early in the project

○ Involve experienced integration specialists

○ Plan for extensive testing of all integration points

4. Scope creep:

○ Establish a formal change control process

○ Regularly review and reaffirm project scope in steering committee meetings

○ Educate stakeholders on the impact of scope changes

5. Inadequate user adoption:

○ Develop a comprehensive training program tailored to different user groups

○ Identify and train super-users to provide peer support

○ Implement a post-go-live support structure

6. Regulatory compliance:

○ Engage compliance experts during the design phase

○ Conduct regular compliance reviews throughout the implementation

○ Plan for a pre-go-live compliance audit

7. System performance:

○ Conduct thorough performance testing under various load scenarios

○ Optimize system configuration for Al Shifa Hospital's specific needs

○ Ensure adequate hardware and network infrastructure

Dr. Khalid nodded approvingly. "This is a comprehensive risk assessment. I appreciate the proactive approach to identifying and addressing potential issues."

Communication Plan and Stakeholder Management

Recognizing the critical role of effective communication in project success, the team dedicated time to developing a robust communication plan and stakeholder management strategy.

Sarah Thompson emphasized the importance of this aspect. "Clear, consistent communication is the lifeline of any successful implementation. We need to ensure that all stakeholders are kept informed and engaged throughout the project."

The team identified key stakeholder groups:

1. Hospital Board of Directors
2. Executive Leadership Team
3. Finance Department Staff
4. Clinical Department Heads
5. IT Department
6. External Auditors
7. Regulatory Bodies
8. Patients and Their Families

For each group, they outlined communication needs, frequency, and channels:

1. Board of Directors:

○ Quarterly progress reports

○ Executive summaries focusing on strategic impact and ROI

2. Executive Leadership Team:

○ Monthly steering committee meetings

○ Weekly status reports

3. Finance Department Staff:

○ Bi-weekly team meetings

○ Regular training sessions and workshops

○ Access to project portal for updates and resources

4. Clinical Department Heads:

○ Monthly update meetings

○ Impact assessments for their departments

5. IT Department:

○ Weekly technical team meetings

○ Collaborative workspace for ongoing technical discussions

6. External Auditors:

○ Quarterly briefings on system changes and compliance measures

7. Regulatory Bodies:

○ As-needed updates on compliance-related system features

○ Invitation to key milestone reviews

8. Patients and Their Families:

○ General announcements about system improvements

○ Updates on any changes to billing processes

The team also agreed on establishing a project portal as a central hub for all project-related communications, documents, and updates.

Change Management Strategy

Recognizing that the success of the implementation heavily depended on user adoption, the team devoted significant attention to developing a comprehensive change management strategy.

Sarah Thompson introduced this crucial aspect, "Change management is often the make-or-break factor in ERP implementations. We need a strategy that addresses the human side of this technological change."

The change management strategy included the following key components:

1. Stakeholder Analysis and Engagement:

○ Identify key influencers and potential resistors

○ Develop targeted engagement plans for different stakeholder groups

2. Communication Campaign:

○ Create a project brand and slogan to build recognition and excitement

○ Develop a multi-channel communication plan (emails, newsletters, town halls, videos)

○ Regularly communicate project benefits, progress, and success stories

3. Training and Education:

○ Conduct a training needs assessment for different user groups

○ Develop role-based training programs

○ Offer multiple training formats (classroom, e-learning, hands-on workshops)

○ Create a library of quick reference guides and FAQs

4. Super User Program:

○ Identify and train super users from each department

○ Empower super users to provide peer support and champion the new system

5. Feedback Mechanisms:

○ Establish channels for users to provide feedback and ask questions

○ Regularly survey users to gauge sentiment and address concerns

6. Leadership Alignment and Visibility:

○ Ensure consistent messaging from leadership about project importance

○ Involve leaders in key project events and communications

7. Rewards and Recognition:

○ Implement a program to recognize staff who embrace the change

○ Celebrate project milestones and early adopters

Dr. Amira Khalid nodded approvingly. "This comprehensive approach to change management will be crucial in ensuring our staff embraces the new system. I particularly like the idea of the super user program – it will give our team a sense of ownership in the project."

Defining Success Criteria and KPIs

As the meeting neared its conclusion, the team turned their attention to defining clear success criteria and Key Performance Indicators (KPIs) for the project. These metrics would serve as benchmarks to evaluate the project's progress and ultimate success.

Rashid Al-Mansoori, the CFO, emphasized the importance of this step. "We need concrete ways to measure whether this implementation is delivering the value we expect. What specific metrics should we be tracking?"

After thoughtful discussion, the team agreed on the following success criteria and KPIs:

1. Financial Process Efficiency:

○ Reduction in month-end close time (Target: 5 days)

○ Decrease in Days Sales Outstanding (Target: 20% reduction)

○ Reduction in manual journal entries (Target: 80% reduction)

2. Data Accuracy and Integrity:

○ Billing accuracy rate (Target: 99%)

○ Reduction in data discrepancies between systems (Target: 95% reduction)

3. Reporting and Analytics:

○ Time to generate key financial reports (Target: Within 24 hours)

○ Increase in available real-time financial dashboards (Target: 10 new dashboards)

4. Compliance and Audit:

○ Compliance with IFRS and local regulations (Target: 100%)

○ Reduction in audit preparation time (Target: 50% reduction)

5. User Adoption and Satisfaction:

○ System usage rates across departments (Target: 95% adoption within 3 months)

○ User satisfaction scores (Target: 80% satisfaction rate)

6. Operational Impact:

○ Reduction in IT support tickets related to financial systems (Target: 60% reduction)

○ Increase in automatic transaction processing (Target: 70% of transactions)

7. Financial Impact:

○ Return on Investment (ROI) of the project (Target: Positive ROI within 24 months)

○ Cost savings from process improvements (Target: 15% reduction in finance operational costs)

Sarah Thompson added, "These KPIs provide a balanced view of the project's impact across various aspects of your financial operations. We'll track these metrics throughout the implementation and beyond to ensure we're delivering the expected value."

Conclusion and Next Steps

As the sun began to set over Dubai, casting a warm glow through the boardroom windows, Dr. Amira Khalid stood up to address the room. The day-long kickoff meeting had been intense but productive, setting a solid foundation for the transformative journey ahead.

"Thank you all for your dedication and input today," she began, her voice filled with determination. "We've accomplished a great deal – defining our objectives, outlining the project scope, establishing timelines, allocating resources, and setting clear success criteria. This Oracle Fusion implementation is more than just a system upgrade; it's a pivotal step towards securing Al Shifa Hospital's financial future and enhancing our ability to serve our patients."

Rashid Al-Mansoori, the CFO, nodded in agreement. "Indeed, the road ahead will be challenging, but I'm confident that with the plans we've put in place today and the expertise of our Oracle partners, we're well-equipped for success."

Sarah Thompson, the Oracle lead, stepped forward. "Thank you for your trust in Oracle. We're committed to making this implementation a success for Al Shifa Hospital. Now, let's outline our immediate next steps to maintain this momentum."

The team agreed on the following action items:

1. Finalize and distribute the Project Charter document within one week
2. Schedule kickoff meetings with individual department heads within two weeks
3. Begin the detailed business process analysis phase next month
4. Set up the project portal and initiate the communication plan immediately
5. Start the change management activities, beginning with a hospital-wide announcement

As the meeting concluded, there was a palpable sense of excitement and purpose in the room. The journey to transform Al Shifa Hospital's financial operations with Oracle Fusion had begun, promising to usher in a new era of efficiency, accuracy, and strategic financial management.

Dr. Khalid's final words resonated with everyone present: "Today, we've laid the foundation for a financial transformation that will enable us to better serve our patients and community. Let's move forward with determination, collaboration, and a shared vision of excellence."

With that, the kickoff meeting adjourned, marking the beginning of Al Shifa Hospital's Oracle Fusion implementation journey. The challenges ahead were significant, but so were the potential rewards. As the team members left the boardroom, there was a shared sense of purpose and optimism about the financial revolution that was about to unfold.

Chapter 4 - General Ledger: The Financial Backbone

Introduction

As Al Shifa Hospital embarked on its journey to implement Oracle Fusion Financials, the team quickly realized that the General Ledger module would serve as the cornerstone of their financial transformation. This chapter explores the critical role of the General Ledger in maintaining accurate financial records and how it forms the foundation for all other financial processes within the hospital.

Understanding the General Ledger

Definition and Purpose

The General Ledger (GL) is the central repository of all financial transactions within an organization. It serves as the primary source of financial data, providing a complete and accurate record of all financial activities. For Al Shifa Hospital, the General Ledger module in Oracle Fusion Financials would become the single source of truth for their financial information.

Dr. Fatima, the hospital's CFO, explained to her team, "Think of the General Ledger as the heart of our financial system. Every transaction, every financial decision we make, will be reflected here. It's crucial that we get this right."

Key Components of the General Ledger

The Oracle Fusion General Ledger module comprises several key components:

1. Chart of Accounts
2. Journal Entries
3. Financial Periods and Year-End Closing
4. Multi-currency Management
5. Consolidation
6. Reporting and Analysis

Implementing the Chart of Accounts

Designing the Structure

One of the first tasks in implementing the General Ledger module was to design an effective Chart of Accounts (COA). The COA is a structured list of all accounts used to record financial transactions and serves as the foundation for financial reporting.

Dr. Fatima worked closely with the Oracle consultants to design a COA that would meet Al Shifa Hospital's specific needs. They considered factors such as:

- Departmental structure
- Service lines
- Funding sources
- Regulatory reporting requirements

The team decided on a segmented account structure that included:

1. Company
2. Department
3. Account
4. Sub-account
5. Project

This structure allowed for detailed tracking and reporting of financial information across various dimensions of the hospital's operations.

Migrating Existing Accounts

With the new COA structure in place, the next challenge was to migrate existing account balances from the old system to Oracle Fusion. This process required careful mapping of old accounts to the new structure and validation of opening balances.

Ahmed, the senior accountant, recalled, "We spent weeks combing through our old accounts, ensuring each one had a proper place in the new system. It was tedious work, but we knew it was crucial for the accuracy of our financial records moving forward."

Journal Entries and Transaction Processing

Streamlining Data Entry

Oracle Fusion's General Ledger module offered Al Shifa Hospital advanced features for journal entry and transaction processing. The system provided:

1. Automated journal creation for recurring entries
2. Spreadsheet integration for bulk uploads
3. Mobile approval workflows for managers

These features significantly reduced manual data entry and improved the accuracy of financial records. Dr. Fatima noted, "The time savings we've achieved in day-to-day accounting tasks have been remarkable. Our team can now focus on more strategic financial analysis instead of getting bogged down in data entry."

Ensuring Data Integrity

To maintain the integrity of financial data, Oracle Fusion implemented several control mechanisms:

1. Journal entry validation rules
2. Segregation of duties
3. Audit trails

These controls helped prevent errors and detect any potential fraudulent activities. The hospital's auditors were particularly impressed with the robust audit trails, which provided a complete history of all changes made to financial records.

Financial Periods and Year-End Closing

Managing Accounting Periods

Oracle Fusion's General Ledger module allowed Al Shifa Hospital to define and manage their financial periods with greater flexibility. The hospital could:

1. Open and close periods as needed
2. Manage multiple periods concurrently
3. Restrict posting to specific periods

This flexibility was particularly useful during month-end and year-end closing processes, allowing the finance team to work more efficiently.

Streamlining Year-End Closing

The year-end closing process, which had previously been a source of stress and long hours for the finance team, was significantly streamlined with Oracle Fusion. The system provided:

1. Automated accruals and deferrals
2. Closing checklist and task management
3. Automated currency revaluation

Mariam, the hospital's controller, shared her experience: "Our first year-end close with Oracle Fusion was a revelation. What used to take us weeks was completed in just a few days, with far fewer errors and much less stress."

Multi-currency Management

Handling Foreign Currencies

As an international hospital in Dubai, Al Shifa frequently dealt with transactions in multiple currencies. Oracle Fusion's General Ledger module provided robust multi-currency management capabilities, including:

1. Real-time currency conversion
2. Automated revaluation of foreign currency balances
3. Detailed foreign currency gain/loss reporting

These features allowed the hospital to accurately track and report on its international operations and investments.

Simplifying Consolidation

For Al Shifa Hospital, which operated several clinics and subsidiaries, the consolidation process had always been complex and time-consuming. Oracle Fusion's General Ledger module simplified this process through:

1. Automated intercompany eliminations
2. Configurable consolidation rules
3. Real-time consolidated reporting

Dr. Fatima remarked, "The ease with which we can now consolidate our financials across all our entities has given us a much clearer picture of our overall financial health. It's been a game-changer for our strategic planning."

Reporting and Analysis

Real-time Financial Visibility

One of the most significant benefits of implementing Oracle Fusion's General Ledger module was the improved financial visibility it provided. The system offered:

1. Real-time financial dashboards
2. Customizable report templates
3. Ad-hoc query capabilities

These tools allowed Al Shifa's management team to access up-to-date financial information at any time, enabling more informed decision-making.

Advanced Analytics

Beyond basic reporting, Oracle Fusion's General Ledger module also provided advanced analytics capabilities, including:

1. Trend analysis
2. Variance reporting
3. What-if scenarios

These features allowed the finance team to dig deeper into the hospital's financial data, uncovering insights that were previously hidden.

Ahmed, who had initially been skeptical about the new system, became one of its biggest advocates. He shared, "The analytics capabilities of Oracle Fusion have transformed how we approach financial analysis. We're now able to spot trends and identify potential issues much earlier than before."

Integration with Other Modules

Seamless Data Flow

While the General Ledger served as the financial backbone, its true power came from its integration with other Oracle Fusion modules. The system allowed for seamless data flow between:

1. Accounts Payable
2. Accounts Receivable
3. Fixed Assets
4. Cash Management

This integration ensured that all financial transactions were accurately reflected in the General Ledger in real-time, providing a complete and up-to-date view of the hospital's financial position.

Enhanced Financial Control

The integrated nature of Oracle Fusion also enhanced financial control by:

1. Eliminating duplicate data entry
2. Reducing reconciliation discrepancies
3. Providing a clear audit trail across modules

Dr. Fatima noted, "The integration between modules has not only improved our efficiency but also significantly reduced the risk of errors. It's given us a level of financial control we've never had before."

Customization and Configuration

Tailoring to Al Shifa's Needs

While Oracle Fusion's General Ledger module came with robust out-of-the-box functionality, the implementation team worked to customize and configure the system to meet Al Shifa Hospital's specific needs. This included:

1. Custom fields for tracking specific healthcare metrics
2. Tailored approval workflows
3. Customized reports for regulatory compliance

The ability to customize the system ensured that Al Shifa could leverage the full power of Oracle Fusion while still addressing their unique requirements as a healthcare provider.

Balancing Customization and Best Practices

Throughout the customization process, the team was careful to balance Al Shifa's specific needs with industry best practices. Dr. Fatima emphasized, "We wanted to leverage thc best practices built into Oracle Fusion while still ensuring the system worked for our specific context. It was a delicate balance, but one that I believe we achieved successfully."

Training and Change Management

Empowering Users

Implementing a new General Ledger system required significant changes to existing processes and workflows. To ensure a smooth transition, Al Shifa invested heavily in training and change management. This included:

1. Role-based training programs
2. Hands-on workshops
3. Creation of a dedicated support team

Mariam, who led the training efforts, shared, "We knew that the success of this implementation would depend on our team's ability to use the system effectively. We made sure everyone had the training and support they needed to feel confident with the new tools."

Overcoming Resistance

As with any major change, there was initial resistance from some team members who were comfortable with the old system. The implementation team addressed this by:

1. Clearly communicating the benefits of the new system
2. Involving key stakeholders in the implementation process
3. Providing ongoing support and encouragement

Over time, even the most skeptical team members came to appreciate the benefits of Oracle Fusion's General Ledger module.

Compliance and Auditing

Meeting Regulatory Requirements

As a healthcare provider, Al Shifa Hospital was subject to strict regulatory requirements. Oracle Fusion's General Ledger module helped the hospital meet these requirements through:

1. Built-in compliance checks
2. Detailed audit trails
3. Configurable security settings

Dr. Fatima noted, "The compliance features in Oracle Fusion have significantly reduced the stress around our annual audits. We now have confidence that our financial records are always audit-ready."

Simplifying the Audit Process

The implementation of Oracle Fusion also simplified the audit process for Al Shifa Hospital. Auditors could now:

1. Access required information more easily
2. Run standard reports directly from the system
3. Trace transactions from source to financial statements

This not only saved time during audits but also reduced the workload on the finance team in preparing for audits.

Challenges and Lessons Learned

Overcoming Implementation Hurdles

While the implementation of Oracle Fusion's General Ledger module was ultimately successful, it was not without its challenges. Some of the key hurdles included:

1. Data migration complexities
2. Initial user resistance
3. Integration with legacy systems

The team overcame these challenges through careful planning, effective communication, and a willingness to adapt their approach as needed.

Key Takeaways

Dr. Fatima reflected on some of the key lessons learned during the implementation:

1. The importance of thorough planning and preparation
2. The need for strong executive sponsorship
3. The value of investing in training and change management
4. The benefits of leveraging system integrators' expertise

She noted, "This implementation taught us a lot about our own processes and capabilities. While it was challenging at times, the lessons we learned have made us stronger as an organization."

Future Outlook

Continuous Improvement

With the successful implementation of Oracle Fusion's General Ledger module, Al Shifa Hospital was well-positioned for future financial success. However, Dr. Fatima and her team recognized that the work was not over. They committed to:

1. Regularly reviewing and optimizing their use of the system
2. Staying up-to-date with new features and updates
3. Continuously training staff to leverage the full capabilities of the system

Expanding Capabilities

Looking to the future, Al Shifa Hospital planned to explore additional capabilities within Oracle Fusion, including:

1. Advanced budgeting and forecasting
2. Predictive analytics
3. Artificial intelligence for anomaly detection

Dr. Fatima shared her vision, "Oracle Fusion's General Ledger module has given us a strong foundation. Now, we're excited to build on that foundation and push the boundaries of what's possible in healthcare financial management."

Conclusion

The implementation of Oracle Fusion's General Ledger module marked a significant milestone in Al Shifa Hospital's financial transformation journey. By providing a robust, integrated, and flexible financial backbone, the system has enabled more accurate record-keeping, improved financial visibility, and enhanced decision-making capabilities.

As Al Shifa Hospital continues to grow and evolve, the General Ledger module will play a crucial role in supporting its financial operations and strategic objectives. The journey of implementation may have been challenging, but the benefits realized have positioned the hospital for long-term financial success in an increasingly complex healthcare landscape.

Chapter 5 - Accounts Receivable: Streamlining Patient Billing

Introduction

As we transition from the General Ledger module, which forms the financial backbone of Al Shifa Hospital's Oracle Fusion implementation, we now turn our attention to a critical component that directly impacts the hospital's cash flow and patient satisfaction: Accounts Receivable. In this chapter, we will explore how the Accounts Receivable module of Oracle Fusion is revolutionizing the way Al Shifa Hospital manages its billing processes, ultimately leading to improved financial health and enhanced patient experiences.

The Importance of Efficient Accounts Receivable in Healthcare

In the complex world of healthcare finance, managing accounts receivable effectively is paramount. For Al Shifa Hospital, like many healthcare institutions, the accounts receivable process involves intricate interactions between patients, insurance companies, and government payers. A well-functioning accounts receivable system ensures that the hospital receives timely payments for services rendered, maintains a healthy cash flow, and can continue providing high-quality care to its patients.

Challenges Faced by Al Shifa Hospital

Before implementing Oracle Fusion, Al Shifa Hospital grappled with several challenges in its accounts receivable processes:

1. **Manual Billing Processes**: The hospital relied heavily on

manual data entry and paper-based billing, leading to errors and delays.

2. **Lack of Real-time Information**: Staff often struggled to access up-to-date patient billing information, resulting in frustrated patients and inefficient customer service.
3. **Delayed Payments**: The hospital experienced significant delays in receiving payments from insurance companies and patients, impacting its cash flow.
4. **Compliance Issues**: Keeping up with changing healthcare regulations and ensuring compliance in billing practices was becoming increasingly difficult.
5. **Limited Reporting Capabilities**: The existing system provided limited insights into receivables performance, making it challenging for management to make informed decisions.

Oracle Fusion Accounts Receivable: A Game-Changer for Al Shifa Hospital

The implementation of Oracle Fusion's Accounts Receivable module marks a significant turning point for Al Shifa Hospital. This powerful tool offers a range of features and capabilities that address the hospital's pain points and pave the way for more efficient and effective billing processes.

Key Features of Oracle Fusion Accounts Receivable

1. Automated Billing Workflows

Oracle Fusion introduces automated billing workflows that significantly reduce manual intervention and the associated errors. The system can automatically generate invoices based on predefined rules and patient data, ensuring accuracy and timeliness in billing.

Example: When a patient is discharged, the system automatically pulls data from various departments (e.g., pharmacy, radiology, laboratory) to create a comprehensive and accurate bill. This process, which previously took days and involved multiple staff members, now happens within hours with minimal human intervention.

2. Real-time Information Access

The module provides real-time access to patient billing information, empowering staff to address patient queries promptly and accurately.

Case Study: Sarah, a billing specialist at Al Shifa Hospital, recalls a situation where a patient called with questions about their bill. Before Oracle Fusion, Sarah would have had to search through multiple systems and potentially call other departments for information. Now, she can access all the necessary details in real-time, providing immediate and accurate answers to the patient's questions.

3. Enhanced Payment Processing

Oracle Fusion streamlines the payment process by offering multiple payment options and automated payment application.

Feature Highlight: The system supports various payment methods, including credit cards, electronic funds transfers, and traditional checks. It also automatically applies payments to the correct invoices, reducing errors and saving time.

4. Robust Compliance Management

The module helps ensure compliance with healthcare regulations by incorporating built-in rules and checks.

Example: When generating bills for services covered by insurance, the system automatically applies the correct coding and pricing based on the latest regulations and agreements with insurance providers.

5. Advanced Reporting and Analytics

Oracle Fusion provides powerful reporting and analytics capabilities, offering valuable insights into receivables performance.

Dashboard Example: The CFO of Al Shifa Hospital now has access to a real-time dashboard showing key metrics such as Days Sales Outstanding (DSO), collection rates, and aging analysis. This information helps in making data-driven decisions to improve financial performance.

Implementing Oracle Fusion Accounts Receivable at Al Shifa Hospital

The implementation of the Accounts Receivable module at Al Shifa Hospital was a carefully planned and executed process. Let's walk through the key stages of this implementation:

1. Assessment and Planning

The first step involved a thorough assessment of Al Shifa Hospital's existing accounts receivable processes. The implementation team, consisting of Oracle consultants and key hospital staff, mapped out current workflows, identified pain points, and defined clear objectives for the new system.

Key Objectives Identified:

- Reduce billing errors by 50%
- Decrease Days Sales Outstanding (DSO) by 20%

- Improve patient satisfaction scores related to billing by 30%

2. System Configuration

Based on the assessment, the Oracle Fusion Accounts Receivable module was configured to meet Al Shifa Hospital's specific needs. This involved setting up:

- Chart of accounts integration with the General Ledger
- Customer master data
- Billing rules and workflows
- Payment terms and methods
- Integration with other hospital systems (e.g., Electronic Health Records)

3. Data Migration

A critical phase of the implementation was migrating existing accounts receivable data to the new system. This process involved:

- Data cleansing to ensure accuracy
- Mapping old data structures to the new Oracle Fusion format
- Rigorous testing to verify data integrity post-migration

Challenge Overcome: During data migration, the team discovered inconsistencies in how patient information was recorded in the old system. They developed a data normalization process to ensure all patient data was consistent and accurate before being imported into Oracle Fusion.

4. User Training

Comprehensive training programs were developed to ensure all relevant staff members could effectively use the new system.

Training Approach:

- Role-based training sessions
- Hands-on workshops
- Creation of user guides and quick reference materials
- Designation of "super users" to provide ongoing support

5. Testing and Go-Live

Before going live, extensive testing was conducted to ensure all components of the Accounts Receivable module were functioning correctly. This included:

- Unit testing of individual components
- Integration testing with other modules and systems
- User acceptance testing involving key stakeholders

The go-live was planned for a weekend to minimize disruption to hospital operations. A dedicated support team was on standby to address any issues that might arise during the transition.

Impact and Benefits of Oracle Fusion Accounts Receivable

The implementation of Oracle Fusion Accounts Receivable has brought about significant improvements in Al Shifa Hospital's billing processes and overall financial health.

1. Improved Billing Accuracy

With automated workflows and real-time data access, billing errors have been significantly reduced.

Result: Billing errors decreased by 60%, surpassing the initial goal of 50%.

2. Faster Collections

The streamlined billing and payment processes have led to quicker collections and improved cash flow.

Result: Days Sales Outstanding (DSO) reduced by 25%, exceeding the target of 20%.

3. Enhanced Patient Satisfaction

Patients now receive accurate bills more quickly and can easily access their billing information.

Result: Patient satisfaction scores related to billing improved by 40%, surpassing the 30% goal.

4. Increased Staff Productivity

Automation of routine tasks has allowed staff to focus on more value-added activities.

Example: The billing team, which previously spent 70% of their time on data entry and reconciliation, now dedicates more time to resolving complex billing issues and improving processes.

5. Better Financial Insights

Advanced reporting capabilities provide management with actionable insights.

Case Study: Using the new analytics tools, the finance team identified a pattern of delayed payments from a particular insurance provider. Armed with this information, they were able to negotiate better terms and improve the payment timeline.

Overcoming Challenges in Accounts Receivable Management

While the implementation of Oracle Fusion Accounts Receivable has been largely successful, Al Shifa Hospital has faced and overcome several challenges in maximizing the system's potential.

1. Adapting to New Workflows

Challenge: Some staff members initially struggled to adapt to the new automated workflows, preferring their familiar manual processes.

Solution: The hospital implemented a mentoring program where tech-savvy "super users" were paired with less confident staff members. This peer-to-peer support accelerated adoption and helped overcome resistance to change.

2. Customization vs. Standardization

Challenge: There was a debate about how much to customize the Oracle Fusion system to match existing processes versus adapting hospital procedures to fit the system's best practices.

Solution: A balanced approach was adopted. Core functionalities were kept standard to benefit from Oracle's built-in best practices, while specific areas crucial to Al Shifa's unique needs were customized.

3. Integration with Legacy Systems

Challenge: Some older systems used in specialized departments were not initially compatible with Oracle Fusion.

Solution: Custom interfaces were developed to ensure seamless data flow between these legacy systems and Oracle Fusion. A phased approach was adopted to gradually replace these systems over time.

4. Data Quality Issues

Challenge: The quality of historical data migrated from the old system sometimes led to inconsistencies in reporting.

Solution: A data governance team was established to continuously monitor and improve data quality. They implemented data validation rules and regular audits to maintain high data integrity.

Best Practices for Maximizing Oracle Fusion Accounts Receivable

Through their implementation journey, Al Shifa Hospital has developed a set of best practices for leveraging Oracle Fusion Accounts Receivable effectively:

1. **Continuous Training**: Regular refresher courses and training

on new features ensure staff are always up-to-date with the system's capabilities.

2. **Process Optimization**: Regularly review and optimize billing processes to take full advantage of the system's automation capabilities.
3. **Leverage Analytics**: Use the advanced analytics tools to identify trends, forecast cash flow, and make data-driven decisions.
4. **Patient Communication**: Utilize the system's capabilities to enhance patient communication regarding bills and payments, improving transparency and satisfaction.
5. **Regular Audits**: Conduct periodic audits of the accounts receivable processes to ensure compliance and identify areas for improvement.
6. **Feedback Loop**: Establish a mechanism for staff to provide feedback on the system, helping identify pain points and potential enhancements.

Future Outlook: Evolving Accounts Receivable at Al Shifa Hospital

As Al Shifa Hospital continues to leverage Oracle Fusion Accounts Receivable, several exciting possibilities for future enhancements are on the horizon:

1. AI-Powered Collections

The hospital is exploring the use of artificial intelligence to optimize collection strategies. This could involve predictive analytics to identify high-risk accounts and suggest personalized collection approaches.

2. Enhanced Patient Portal Integration

Plans are underway to further integrate the accounts receivable system with the patient portal, allowing patients greater visibility and control over their billing and payment processes.

3. Blockchain for Claims Processing

Al Shifa Hospital is considering the potential of blockchain technology to streamline claims processing with insurance providers, potentially reducing processing times and improving accuracy.

4. Mobile Solutions for Staff

To further improve efficiency, the hospital is looking into mobile solutions that would allow staff to access and update accounts receivable information on-the-go.

Conclusion

The implementation of Oracle Fusion Accounts Receivable has marked a significant milestone in Al Shifa Hospital's journey towards financial excellence. By streamlining billing processes, improving accuracy, and providing powerful insights, the system has not only enhanced the hospital's financial health but also contributed to better patient experiences.

As we move forward, the Accounts Receivable module will continue to play a crucial role in Al Shifa Hospital's financial operations. Its integration with other Oracle Fusion modules, particularly Accounts Payable, which we will explore in the next chapter, creates a comprehensive financial ecosystem that positions the hospital for sustained success in an ever-evolving healthcare landscape.

The transformation achieved in accounts receivable management serves as a testament to the power of innovative technology solutions in addressing complex healthcare financial challenges. As Al Shifa Hospital continues to evolve and adapt, the foundation laid by Oracle Fusion Accounts Receivable will undoubtedly support its mission of providing exceptional care while maintaining financial stability.

Chapter 6 - Accounts Payable: Optimizing Vendor Management

Introduction: The Critical Role of Accounts Payable in Hospital Finance

As Al Shifa Hospital continues its journey towards financial transformation with Oracle Fusion, the Accounts Payable (AP) module emerges as a crucial component in optimizing vendor management and streamlining payment processes. This chapter delves into the intricacies of the AP module, demonstrating its potential to revolutionize the hospital's relationship with suppliers and enhance overall financial efficiency.

Understanding Accounts Payable in Healthcare

The Unique Challenges of Hospital AP

In the healthcare sector, Accounts Payable faces distinct challenges that set it apart from other industries. Al Shifa Hospital, like many healthcare institutions, grapples with:

1. High volume of transactions: From medical supplies to equipment maintenance, hospitals process an enormous number of invoices daily.
2. Diverse vendor ecosystem: Healthcare providers work with a wide range of suppliers, from pharmaceutical companies to medical device manufacturers and service providers.
3. Stringent regulatory requirements: Compliance with healthcare regulations adds an extra layer of complexity to AP processes.
4. Time-sensitive payments: Delayed payments can impact

critical supply chains, potentially affecting patient care.

Oracle Fusion AP Module: A Game-Changer for Al Shifa Hospital

Key Features and Capabilities

The Oracle Fusion AP module offers a comprehensive suite of tools designed to address the unique needs of healthcare institutions like Al Shifa Hospital. Some of the key features include:

1. Automated invoice processing
2. Intelligent document recognition
3. Seamless integration with procurement and general ledger
4. Robust vendor management tools
5. Advanced payment scheduling and optimization
6. Comprehensive reporting and analytics

Streamlining Invoice Processing

From Paper to Digital: Embracing Automation

One of the most significant pain points for Al Shifa Hospital's AP department was the manual processing of invoices. The Oracle Fusion AP module introduces a paradigm shift by automating this process:

1. Intelligent Document Recognition (IDR): The system can automatically extract key information from invoices, regardless of format or layout.
2. Three-way matching: Invoices are automatically matched with purchase orders and receiving reports, significantly reducing errors and processing time.
3. Exception handling: The system flags discrepancies for human

review, allowing staff to focus on high-value tasks rather than routine data entry.

Case Study: Al Shifa's Invoice Processing Transformation

Before implementing Oracle Fusion, Al Shifa Hospital's AP team processed an average of 500 invoices per day, with each invoice taking approximately 15 minutes to process manually. This resulted in:

- 125 staff hours per day dedicated to invoice processing
- Frequent errors and discrepancies
- Delayed payments and strained vendor relationships

After implementing Oracle Fusion AP:

- Invoice processing time reduced to an average of 2 minutes per invoice
- 90% of invoices processed without human intervention
- Staff hours dedicated to invoice processing reduced to 16 per day
- Error rates decreased by 95%

This transformation allowed Al Shifa to reallocate staff to more strategic financial management tasks, improving overall departmental efficiency.

Enhancing Vendor Relationships

Centralized Vendor Management

The Oracle Fusion AP module provides Al Shifa Hospital with a centralized platform for managing vendor information, contracts, and interactions. This centralization offers several benefits:

1. Single source of truth: All vendor information is stored in one place, ensuring consistency across departments.
2. Self-service vendor portal: Suppliers can update their own information, submit invoices, and check payment status, reducing the burden on AP staff.
3. Performance tracking: The hospital can easily monitor vendor performance, identify preferred suppliers, and negotiate better terms based on data-driven insights.

Improved Communication and Collaboration

With Oracle Fusion AP, Al Shifa Hospital has been able to significantly enhance its communication with vendors:

1. Automated notifications: Vendors receive real-time updates on invoice and payment status.
2. Dispute resolution: The system provides a structured process for addressing discrepancies, ensuring timely resolution of issues.
3. Vendor scorecards: Regular performance evaluations help maintain high-quality supplier relationships.

Optimizing Payment Processes

Strategic Payment Scheduling

Oracle Fusion AP empowers Al Shifa Hospital to optimize its payment processes, balancing cash flow management with vendor satisfaction:

1. Dynamic discounting: The system identifies opportunities for early payment discounts, allowing the hospital to save money while supporting vendors' cash flow needs.
2. Payment date optimization: Payments are scheduled to maximize working capital while meeting vendor terms.
3. Multiple payment methods: The system supports various payment methods, including ACH, wire transfers, and virtual card payments, providing flexibility and potential rebate opportunities.

Case Study: Al Shifa's Payment Optimization Journey

Prior to Oracle Fusion, Al Shifa Hospital struggled with:

- Missed early payment discounts, estimated at $500,000 annually
- Late payment penalties averaging $100,000 per year
- Strained relationships with key suppliers due to payment delays

After implementing Oracle Fusion AP:

- Captured 95% of available early payment discounts, resulting in $475,000 annual savings

- Eliminated late payment penalties
- Improved vendor satisfaction scores by 40%

Ensuring Compliance and Control

Built-in Compliance Features

For Al Shifa Hospital, maintaining regulatory compliance is paramount. Oracle Fusion AP offers robust compliance features:

1. Segregation of duties: The system enforces strict role-based access controls, preventing fraud and ensuring proper oversight.
2. Audit trails: Every transaction and system change is logged, providing a complete audit history.
3. Configurable approval workflows: Custom approval hierarchies can be set up to match the hospital's internal control requirements.

Fraud Prevention and Detection

Oracle Fusion AP includes advanced fraud detection capabilities:

1. Duplicate payment detection: The system automatically flags potential duplicate invoices or payments.
2. Vendor validation: Automatic checks against sanction lists and other databases help prevent payments to unauthorized entities.
3. Anomaly detection: Machine learning algorithms identify unusual patterns in invoice or payment data, alerting staff to potential fraud.

Leveraging Data for Strategic Decision-Making

Comprehensive Reporting and Analytics

The real power of Oracle Fusion AP lies in its ability to provide Al Shifa Hospital with actionable insights:

1. Customizable dashboards: Finance leaders can access real-time AP metrics at a glance.
2. Spend analysis: The system provides detailed breakdowns of spending by category, department, and vendor.
3. Cash flow forecasting: Advanced predictive analytics help the hospital better manage its working capital.

Data-Driven Vendor Strategies

With Oracle Fusion AP, Al Shifa Hospital can develop more strategic vendor relationships:

1. Consolidation opportunities: The system identifies areas where the hospital can consolidate vendors to negotiate better terms.
2. Risk assessment: Vendor performance data helps identify potential supply chain risks.
3. Contract optimization: Analysis of spending patterns and vendor performance informs contract negotiations.

Integration with Other Oracle Fusion Modules

Seamless Financial Ecosystem

The power of Oracle Fusion AP is amplified by its integration with other modules:

1. Procurement: Seamless flow of information from purchase orders to invoice processing.
2. General Ledger: Automatic posting of AP transactions ensures up-to-date financial records.
3. Cash Management: Integration with payment processes optimizes cash flow management.

Challenges and Solutions in AP Transformation

Overcoming Resistance to Change

Implementing Oracle Fusion AP at Al Shifa Hospital was not without its challenges:

1. Staff apprehension: Many AP team members were initially hesitant about the new system.
   Solution: Comprehensive training programs and change management initiatives helped ease the transition.
2. Vendor adoption: Some suppliers were slow to adopt the new self-service portal.
   Solution: Al Shifa provided vendor training sessions and highlighted the benefits of the new system, such as faster payments and improved communication.
3. Data migration: Transferring historical vendor and invoice data to the new system posed challenges.
   Solution: A phased approach to data migration, coupled with rigorous data cleansing and validation processes, ensured a smooth transition.

Future of AP at Al Shifa Hospital

Continuous Improvement and Innovation

As Al Shifa Hospital becomes more proficient with Oracle Fusion AP, several areas for future enhancement have been identified:

1. AI-powered invoice processing: Exploring advanced machine learning capabilities to further automate invoice handling.
2. Blockchain for supply chain transparency: Investigating the potential of blockchain technology to enhance traceability and security in the supply chain.
3. Predictive analytics for vendor management: Developing models to predict vendor performance and potential supply chain disruptions.

Conclusion: A New Era of Financial Efficiency

The implementation of Oracle Fusion AP has marked the beginning of a new era in vendor management and financial efficiency for Al Shifa Hospital. By streamlining invoice processing, enhancing vendor relationships, optimizing payment processes, and leveraging data-driven insights, the hospital has not only improved its financial operations but also positioned itself for sustainable growth and improved patient care.

As we move forward to explore the Fixed Assets module in the next chapter, it's clear that the transformation of Al Shifa Hospital's financial landscape is well underway, with each Oracle Fusion module contributing to a more efficient, transparent, and strategically-aligned financial ecosystem.

Chapter 7 - Fixed Assets: Managing Hospital Equipment

Introduction

As we transition from the previous chapter on optimizing vendor management through Accounts Payable, we now turn our attention to another critical aspect of hospital finance: managing fixed assets. For Al Shifa Hospital, like many healthcare institutions, fixed assets represent a significant portion of its overall value and are essential for providing quality patient care. In this chapter, we will explore how Oracle Fusion's Fixed Assets module can revolutionize the way Al Shifa Hospital tracks, maintains, and optimizes its valuable medical equipment and infrastructure.

The Importance of Fixed Asset Management in Healthcare

Defining Fixed Assets in a Hospital Setting

In the context of Al Shifa Hospital, fixed assets encompass a wide range of items, including:

1. Medical equipment (e.g., MRI machines, CT scanners, X-ray machines)
2. Surgical instruments and tools
3. Hospital beds and furniture
4. IT infrastructure (computers, servers, networking equipment)
5. Buildings and facilities
6. Vehicles (ambulances, patient transport vans)

Effective management of these assets is crucial for several reasons:

1. Financial accuracy: Fixed assets represent a significant investment and impact the hospital's financial statements.
2. Regulatory compliance: Proper tracking and reporting of assets are often required by healthcare regulations.
3. Operational efficiency: Knowing the location, condition, and maintenance status of equipment ensures smooth operations.
4. Patient care quality: Well-maintained and properly managed equipment contributes to better patient outcomes.

Challenges in Traditional Fixed Asset Management

Before implementing Oracle Fusion, Al Shifa Hospital faced numerous challenges in managing its fixed assets:

1. Manual tracking: Reliance on spreadsheets and paper-based records led to inaccuracies and inefficiencies.
2. Lack of real-time visibility: It was difficult to get an up-to-date view of asset locations and status.
3. Depreciation calculations: Complex depreciation schedules were prone to errors when managed manually.
4. Maintenance scheduling: Keeping track of equipment maintenance was challenging, leading to potential downtime and safety issues.
5. Audit trails: Maintaining a clear history of asset transactions and changes was cumbersome.
6. Reporting difficulties: Generating comprehensive reports for management and regulatory purposes was time-consuming and often inaccurate.

Introducing Oracle Fusion Fixed Assets Module

Overview of Key Features

Oracle Fusion's Fixed Assets module offers a comprehensive solution to address these challenges. Some of its key features include:

1. Asset tracking and management
2. Automated depreciation calculations
3. Maintenance scheduling and tracking
4. Integration with other financial modules
5. Robust reporting and analytics capabilities
6. Mobile access for on-the-go asset management

Let's explore how each of these features benefits Al Shifa Hospital.

Asset Tracking and Management

Centralized Asset Register

One of the primary benefits of Oracle Fusion's Fixed Assets module is the creation of a centralized asset register. This digital repository contains detailed information about each asset, including:

1. Asset description and classification
2. Purchase date and cost
3. Current location
4. Assigned department or user
5. Maintenance history
6. Depreciation schedule
7. Expected useful life

For Al Shifa Hospital, this means that every piece of medical equipment, from large imaging machines to small surgical instruments, can be easily tracked and managed from a single system.

Asset Tagging and Barcoding

To facilitate accurate tracking, Oracle Fusion supports asset tagging and barcoding. Each asset is assigned a unique identifier, which can be scanned using mobile devices. This feature proves particularly useful for Al Shifa Hospital's biomedical engineering team, who can quickly locate and identify equipment for maintenance or repairs.

Real-time Asset Tracking

The ability to track assets in real-time is a game-changer for Al Shifa Hospital. With Oracle Fusion, staff can:

1. Locate equipment quickly, reducing time wasted searching for items
2. Monitor the movement of assets between departments
3. Identify underutilized equipment for potential reallocation
4. Prevent loss or theft of valuable medical devices

Automated Depreciation Calculations

Configurable Depreciation Methods

Oracle Fusion's Fixed Assets module supports various depreciation methods, allowing Al Shifa Hospital to apply the most appropriate method for each asset type. These methods include:

1. Straight-line depreciation
2. Declining balance

3. Sum-of-the-years' digits
4. Units of production

The system automatically calculates depreciation based on the chosen method, asset cost, and useful life, ensuring accuracy and consistency across all assets.

Handling Complex Scenarios

Healthcare equipment often involves complex depreciation scenarios. Oracle Fusion can handle situations such as:

1. Partial year depreciation for assets acquired mid-year
2. Changes in depreciation methods or useful life estimates
3. Impairment of assets due to technological obsolescence
4. Disposal or retirement of assets before the end of their useful life

This flexibility allows Al Shifa Hospital to accurately reflect the true value of its assets in financial statements, supporting better decision-making and financial planning.

Maintenance Scheduling and Tracking

Preventive Maintenance Planning

Regular maintenance is crucial for ensuring the longevity and reliability of medical equipment. Oracle Fusion's Fixed Assets module includes features for:

1. Setting up maintenance schedules based on time intervals or usage
2. Generating automatic notifications for upcoming

maintenance tasks
3. Tracking the completion of maintenance activities
4. Recording maintenance costs and associating them with specific assets

For Al Shifa Hospital, this means reduced equipment downtime, improved patient safety, and extended asset lifespans.

Integration with Work Order Systems

Oracle Fusion can integrate with the hospital's existing work order system, streamlining the process of requesting and tracking equipment repairs. When a piece of equipment requires maintenance:

1. A work order is automatically generated in the system
2. The biomedical engineering team is notified
3. The asset's status is updated to reflect that it's undergoing maintenance
4. Upon completion, the asset record is updated with details of the work performed

This integration ensures that all maintenance activities are properly documented and easily accessible for future reference.

Integration with Other Financial Modules

Seamless Data Flow

One of the key advantages of Oracle Fusion is its integrated approach to financial management. The Fixed Assets module seamlessly connects with other modules, including:

1. General Ledger: Automatically posting depreciation entries

and asset-related transactions
2. Accounts Payable: Linking asset purchases to vendor invoices
3. Procurement: Streamlining the process of acquiring new assets

For Al Shifa Hospital, this integration eliminates the need for manual data entry across multiple systems, reducing errors and improving overall financial accuracy.

Impact on Financial Reporting

The integration of fixed assets data with the General Ledger ensures that Al Shifa Hospital's financial statements accurately reflect:

1. The current value of assets after depreciation
2. Gains or losses from asset disposals
3. Maintenance and repair expenses associated with specific assets

This level of detail supports more informed financial decision-making and helps the hospital optimize its asset management strategies.

Robust Reporting and Analytics Capabilities

Standard and Custom Reports

Oracle Fusion's Fixed Assets module offers a wide range of standard reports, including:

1. Asset register reports
2. Depreciation schedules
3. Asset acquisition and disposal reports

4. Maintenance history reports
5. Asset valuation reports

Additionally, Al Shifa Hospital can create custom reports tailored to its specific needs, such as:

1. Equipment utilization rates by department
2. Comparison of maintenance costs across different asset types
3. Projected equipment replacement schedules based on useful life estimates

Data Visualization and Dashboards

To make complex asset data more accessible, Oracle Fusion provides powerful visualization tools. Al Shifa Hospital's management can use interactive dashboards to:

1. View the distribution of assets across departments
2. Monitor depreciation trends over time
3. Analyze maintenance costs and identify areas for potential cost savings
4. Track key performance indicators related to asset management

These visual insights enable quicker decision-making and help identify potential issues before they become critical.

Mobile Access for On-the-Go Asset Management

Empowering Field Staff

Oracle Fusion's mobile capabilities are particularly beneficial for Al Shifa Hospital's biomedical engineering team and other staff who need to manage assets on the move. Using smartphones or tablets, they can:

1. Scan asset tags to access detailed information
2. Update asset locations in real-time
3. Log maintenance activities as they're performed
4. Capture photos of assets for documentation purposes
5. Access maintenance manuals and asset histories while in the field

This mobile functionality improves efficiency and ensures that asset data is always up-to-date, regardless of where the work is being performed.

Implementing Oracle Fusion Fixed Assets at Al Shifa Hospital

Project Phases

The implementation of Oracle Fusion's Fixed Assets module at Al Shifa Hospital was carried out in several phases:

1. Assessment and planning: Evaluating current asset management practices and defining project objectives
2. Data preparation: Cleansing and organizing existing asset data for migration
3. System configuration: Setting up the Fixed Assets module to align with hospital policies and procedures

4. Data migration: Transferring asset records from legacy systems to Oracle Fusion
5. Testing and validation: Ensuring accuracy of migrated data and functionality of the new system
6. User training: Educating staff on how to use the new Fixed Assets module
7. Go-live and support: Transitioning to the new system and providing ongoing assistance

Challenges and Solutions

During the implementation, Al Shifa Hospital encountered several challenges:

1. Data quality issues: Many asset records in the legacy system were incomplete or inaccurate. Solution: A dedicated team was assigned to clean and verify data before migration.
2. Resistance to change: Some staff members were hesitant to adopt the new system. Solution: Change management strategies were employed, including regular communication and hands-on training sessions.
3. Integration with existing systems: Connecting Oracle Fusion with the hospital's work order system required custom development. Solution: Oracle consultants worked closely with the hospital's IT team to create seamless integrations.
4. Customizing depreciation methods: Some medical equipment required specialized depreciation calculations. Solution: Oracle Fusion's flexibility allowed for the creation of custom depreciation methods to meet these specific needs.

Benefits Realized by Al Shifa Hospital

After implementing Oracle Fusion's Fixed Assets module, Al Shifa Hospital experienced numerous benefits:

1. Improved accuracy: Automated processes reduced errors in asset tracking and depreciation calculations.
2. Enhanced visibility: Real-time asset tracking provided a clear picture of equipment location and status.
3. Cost savings: Better maintenance scheduling extended asset lifespans and reduced unexpected breakdowns.
4. Increased efficiency: Staff spent less time on manual data entry and more time on value-added activities.
5. Stronger compliance: Accurate asset records and audit trails simplified regulatory reporting.
6. Informed decision-making: Comprehensive reporting and analytics supported data-driven asset management strategies.
7. Optimized utilization: Improved tracking helped identify underutilized equipment for reallocation.
8. Streamlined audits: Easy access to detailed asset histories and transaction records simplified the audit process.

Case Study: Improving MRI Machine Management

To illustrate the impact of Oracle Fusion's Fixed Assets module, let's examine how it improved the management of Al Shifa Hospital's MRI machines:

Before implementation:

- Tracking maintenance schedules was challenging, leading to occasional missed services

- Depreciation calculations were done manually, resulting in occasional errors

- Utilization rates were difficult to measure accurately

- Costs associated with each machine were not clearly linked in financial reports

After implementation:

- Automated maintenance notifications ensured timely servicing, reducing downtime

- Accurate depreciation calculations improved financial reporting

- Real-time tracking of machine usage provided insights into utilization patterns

- All costs (maintenance, repairs, upgrades) were easily associated with each machine, providing a clear picture of total ownership costs

As a result, Al Shifa Hospital was able to optimize its MRI machine usage, reduce maintenance costs, and make more informed decisions about future equipment purchases.

Future Enhancements and Opportunities

As Al Shifa Hospital continues to leverage Oracle Fusion's Fixed Assets module, several opportunities for further enhancement have been identified:

1. IoT integration: Exploring the possibility of connecting medical equipment directly to the asset management system for real-time performance monitoring and predictive maintenance.
2. AI-powered predictive analytics: Utilizing machine learning

algorithms to predict equipment failures and optimize maintenance schedules.

3. Expanded mobile capabilities: Developing custom mobile apps for specific asset management tasks tailored to Al Shifa Hospital's workflows.
4. Enhanced integration with patient care systems: Linking asset data with patient records to track equipment usage at the individual patient level, supporting more detailed cost analysis and quality improvement initiatives.
5. Sustainability tracking: Incorporating features to monitor and report on the environmental impact of assets, supporting Al Shifa Hospital's sustainability goals.

Conclusion

The implementation of Oracle Fusion's Fixed Assets module has transformed the way Al Shifa Hospital manages its valuable medical equipment and infrastructure. By providing a centralized, automated system for asset tracking, depreciation, and maintenance management, Oracle Fusion has enabled the hospital to improve accuracy, increase efficiency, and make more informed decisions about its assets.

The benefits realized extend beyond just financial management, impacting patient care quality, regulatory compliance, and operational efficiency. As Al Shifa Hospital continues to explore the full potential of the Fixed Assets module, it is well-positioned to further optimize its asset management practices and drive continued improvements in healthcare delivery.

As we move forward to the next chapter, we will explore how Oracle Fusion's Cash Management module complements these asset management capabilities, further enhancing Al Shifa Hospital's financial control and stability.

Chapter 8 - Cash Management: Enhancing Financial Control

Introduction

As Al Shifa Hospital continues its journey towards financial transformation with Oracle Fusion, one crucial aspect of its financial operations comes into focus: cash management. In this chapter, we'll explore how the Cash Management module of Oracle Fusion plays a pivotal role in maintaining liquidity and financial stability for the hospital.

The Importance of Cash Management in Healthcare

In the fast-paced world of healthcare, effective cash management is not just a financial necessity; it's a lifeline that ensures the smooth operation of critical services. For Al Shifa Hospital, managing cash flow efficiently means being able to:

1. Meet payroll obligations for its dedicated staff
2. Purchase essential medical supplies and equipment
3. Invest in cutting-edge technologies and treatments
4. Maintain and upgrade facilities
5. Handle unexpected expenses or emergencies

Current Challenges at Al Shifa Hospital

Before implementing Oracle Fusion's Cash Management module, Al Shifa Hospital faced several challenges:

1. Limited visibility into real-time cash positions
2. Difficulty in forecasting cash flow accurately
3. Manual reconciliation processes that were time-consuming

and error-prone
4. Inefficient bank communication and transaction processing
5. Lack of centralized control over cash-related activities

Dr. Fatima, the CFO of Al Shifa Hospital, explains, "We were constantly playing catch-up with our cash management. It felt like we were always one step behind, reacting to financial situations rather than proactively managing them."

Oracle Fusion Cash Management: An Overview

The Cash Management module of Oracle Fusion offers a comprehensive solution to address these challenges. It provides a centralized platform for managing all cash-related activities, from bank reconciliation to cash positioning and forecasting.

Key features of the module include:

1. Real-time cash visibility
2. Automated bank statement reconciliation
3. Cash flow forecasting and modeling
4. Bank account management
5. Payment processing and bank connectivity
6. Cash pooling and in-house banking

Implementing Cash Management at Al Shifa Hospital

Step 1: Setting Up Bank Accounts

The first step in implementing the Cash Management module was to set up and configure all of Al Shifa Hospital's bank accounts within the system. This process involved:

1. Gathering information on all existing bank accounts

2. Defining bank account structures and hierarchies
3. Setting up bank account signatories and approval workflows
4. Configuring bank statement formats for automated imports

Ahmed, the IT lead for the project, recalls, "It was a meticulous process, but it laid the foundation for everything that followed. We had to ensure every account was accurately represented in the system."

Step 2: Establishing Bank Connectivity

To enable real-time visibility and automated processes, Al Shifa Hospital needed to establish secure connections with its banks. This involved:

1. Setting up SWIFT connectivity for international transactions
2. Implementing local electronic banking protocols for domestic transactions
3. Configuring security measures to protect sensitive financial data

Dr. Fatima notes, "The ability to connect directly with our banks was a game-changer. It meant we could finally have up-to-the-minute information on our cash positions."

Step 3: Automating Bank Statement Reconciliation

One of the most time-consuming tasks for Al Shifa's finance team was reconciling bank statements. Oracle Fusion's Cash Management module automated this process:

1. Configuring rules for automatic matching of transactions
2. Setting up exception handling processes for unmatched items
3. Implementing approval workflows for reconciliation

Aisha, the head of accounting, shares, "What used to take us days now happens in minutes. It's not just faster; it's also more accurate and allows us to focus on analyzing the data rather than just processing it."

Step 4: Implementing Cash Positioning and Forecasting

With the foundational elements in place, Al Shifa Hospital could now leverage the power of Oracle Fusion for cash positioning and forecasting:

1. Setting up cash position worksheets to provide real-time visibility
2. Configuring cash forecast templates
3. Integrating with other Oracle Fusion modules (AR, AP, GL) for comprehensive forecasting
4. Establishing cash flow modeling scenarios

Dr. Fatima explains, "For the first time, we have a clear picture of our cash position not just for today, but for weeks and months ahead. It's transformed how we make financial decisions."

Step 5: Optimizing Payment Processing

The Cash Management module also allowed Al Shifa Hospital to streamline its payment processes:

1. Centralizing payment approvals
2. Implementing electronic payment methods
3. Setting up payment factories for efficient processing
4. Configuring rules for payment prioritization

Ahmed notes, "The efficiency gains in our payment processes were immediate. We're now able to process payments faster, more securely, and with better control."

Key Benefits Realized

As Al Shifa Hospital fully implemented and adopted the Cash Management module, several key benefits emerged:

1. Enhanced Visibility: Real-time access to cash positions across all bank accounts provided a clear picture of the hospital's financial status at any given moment.
2. Improved Forecasting: The ability to create accurate cash flow forecasts enabled better financial planning and decision-making.
3. Increased Efficiency: Automation of bank reconciliations and payment processes freed up significant time for the finance team to focus on more strategic tasks.
4. Better Control: Centralized management of cash-related activities improved control and reduced the risk of errors or fraud.
5. Optimized Cash Utilization: With better visibility and forecasting, Al Shifa Hospital could optimize its cash utilization, ensuring funds were always available when needed while maximizing returns on excess cash.
6. Reduced Bank Fees: Streamlined processes and better bank account management led to a reduction in bank fees and charges.
7. Enhanced Compliance: Improved tracking and reporting capabilities helped ensure compliance with financial regulations and internal policies.

Challenges Faced and Overcome

While the implementation of the Cash Management module brought significant benefits, it wasn't without its challenges:

1. Data Migration: Transferring historical cash management data to the new system proved complex. The team overcame this by developing a phased migration approach and conducting thorough data validation at each stage.
2. User Adoption: Some staff members were initially resistant to the new system. Comprehensive training programs and ongoing support helped ease the transition.
3. Bank Cooperation: Establishing direct bank connections required cooperation from multiple banking partners. Dr. Fatima's team worked closely with each bank to ensure smooth integration.
4. System Integration: Ensuring seamless integration with other financial modules required careful planning and testing. The IT team worked diligently to resolve any integration issues that arose.

Case Study: Managing a Cash Flow Crisis

Six months after fully implementing the Cash Management module, Al Shifa Hospital faced an unexpected cash flow crisis due to delayed payments from a major insurance provider. Thanks to the new system, the finance team was able to:

1. Quickly identify the impact of the delayed payments on cash flow
2. Generate accurate forecasts to understand the extent of the shortfall
3. Model various scenarios to determine the best course of action
4. Optimize payment schedules to prioritize critical expenses

5. Identify and utilize short-term investment funds to cover the gap

Dr. Fatima reflects, "In the past, a situation like this would have caught us off guard and potentially led to serious financial strain. With Oracle Fusion, we were able to navigate the crisis with confidence and precision."

Future Enhancements and Opportunities

As Al Shifa Hospital continues to leverage the Cash Management module, several opportunities for further enhancement have been identified:

1. Advanced Analytics: Implementing predictive analytics to further improve cash flow forecasting accuracy.
2. AI-Powered Reconciliation: Exploring the use of artificial intelligence to handle complex reconciliation scenarios automatically.
3. Treasury Management: Expanding the use of the module to include more advanced treasury management functions.
4. Global Expansion: As the hospital considers expanding its operations internationally, the Cash Management module will play a crucial role in managing multi-currency transactions and cross-border cash pooling.

Best Practices for Cash Management

Through their experience with Oracle Fusion's Cash Management module, Al Shifa Hospital has developed a set of best practices:

1. Centralize cash management activities for better control and visibility
2. Regularly review and update cash flow forecasts

3. Implement robust approval workflows for all cash-related transactions
4. Continuously monitor bank fees and charges to optimize banking relationships
5. Regularly reconcile all bank accounts to ensure accuracy
6. Leverage cash pooling to optimize liquidity across the organization
7. Implement strong security measures to protect financial data and transactions
8. Provide ongoing training to staff to ensure maximum utilization of the system's capabilities

The Road Ahead

As Al Shifa Hospital continues its financial transformation journey with Oracle Fusion, the Cash Management module stands as a cornerstone of its improved financial operations. Dr. Fatima summarizes, "The visibility, control, and efficiency we've gained through this implementation have been transformative. We're now in a much stronger position to manage our finances proactively and support the hospital's mission of providing exceptional healthcare."

With a solid foundation in cash management now in place, Al Shifa Hospital is well-equipped to face future financial challenges and opportunities. The journey of financial transformation continues, but with Oracle Fusion's Cash Management module, the hospital has taken a significant step towards ensuring its financial health and stability.

Conclusion

The implementation of Oracle Fusion's Cash Management module at Al Shifa Hospital demonstrates the profound impact that advanced financial technology can have on healthcare organizations. By providing real-time visibility, automating key processes, and enabling sophisticated forecasting and modeling, the module has empowered the hospital to take control of its cash flow and make more informed financial decisions.

As we move forward in our exploration of Al Shifa Hospital's Oracle Fusion implementation journey, we'll next examine the challenges faced during the implementation process and how the team overcame them. These lessons will provide valuable insights for other organizations considering similar financial transformations.

Chapter 9 - Implementation Challenges: Overcoming Hurdles

Introduction

As Al Shifa Hospital embarked on its journey to implement Oracle Fusion Financials, the excitement of transformation was palpable. However, like any major technological overhaul, the path to success was not without its obstacles. This chapter delves into the various challenges faced by the hospital's implementation team and how they navigated through these hurdles to ensure a successful Oracle Fusion deployment.

Resistance to Change

One of the first and most significant challenges encountered was the natural resistance to change among hospital staff. Many employees, particularly those who had been with Al Shifa for years, were comfortable with the existing systems and processes.

Identifying the Root Causes

The implementation team, led by Chief Information Officer (CIO) Fatima Al-Mansouri, conducted a series of surveys and focus groups to understand the underlying reasons for this resistance. They discovered several key factors:

1. Fear of job obsolescence
2. Comfort with existing processes
3. Lack of understanding of the new system's benefits
4. Concerns about increased workload during the transition

Strategies to Overcome Resistance

To address these concerns, the team developed a multi-pronged approach:

1. **Clear Communication**: Regular town hall meetings were organized to explain the benefits of Oracle Fusion and how it would positively impact each department.
2. **Change Champions**: The team identified influential employees from various departments and trained them as "Change Champions" to advocate for the new system.
3. **Hands-on Demonstrations**: Interactive sessions were conducted to showcase the user-friendly interface and efficiency gains of Oracle Fusion.
4. **Job Security Assurances**: Hospital leadership communicated that the goal was to enhance productivity, not reduce headcount.

Technical Integration Complexities

The technical aspect of integrating Oracle Fusion with existing hospital systems posed another significant challenge. Al Shifa Hospital had a complex ecosystem of legacy applications, including an outdated Electronic Health Record (EHR) system and various departmental software.

Identifying Integration Points

The IT team, working closely with Oracle consultants, mapped out all the critical integration points between Oracle Fusion and existing systems. Key areas included:

1. Patient billing data flow from the EHR to Oracle Fusion

Accounts Receivable

2. Inventory management system integration with Oracle Fusion Procurement
3. Payroll system connection to Oracle Fusion Human Capital Management

Overcoming Technical Hurdles

To address these technical challenges, the team employed several strategies:

1. **Custom API Development**: Where standard integrations were not available, the team developed custom APIs to ensure seamless data flow.
2. **Phased Integration Approach**: Instead of attempting a "big bang" integration, the team adopted a phased approach, starting with less critical systems and gradually moving to core applications.
3. **Extensive Testing**: Rigorous testing protocols were established, including unit testing, integration testing, and user acceptance testing, to identify and resolve issues early.
4. **Contingency Planning**: Fallback plans were developed for each integration point in case of unexpected issues during go-live.

Data Migration Challenges

Migrating years of financial and operational data from legacy systems to Oracle Fusion presented its own set of challenges. The data was often inconsistent, incomplete, or stored in incompatible formats.

Data Quality Assessment

The first step in addressing this challenge was a comprehensive data quality assessment. The team discovered several issues:

1. Duplicate patient records
2. Inconsistent vendor information across departments
3. Incomplete historical financial data
4. Varying data formats and coding systems

Strategies for Successful Data Migration

To ensure a smooth and accurate data migration, the team implemented the following strategies:

1. **Data Cleansing**: A dedicated team was assigned to clean and standardize data before migration, focusing on critical elements like patient demographics and financial records.
2. **Automated Data Validation**: Custom scripts were developed to automatically check for data inconsistencies and flag potential issues.
3. **Phased Migration**: Data was migrated in phases, starting with historical data and moving towards more recent and critical information.
4. **Parallel Run**: For a period, both the old and new systems were run in parallel to ensure data accuracy and completeness in Oracle Fusion.

Training and Skill Gap

Implementing a sophisticated system like Oracle Fusion required a significant upgrade in the skill set of Al Shifa Hospital's staff. Many employees were unfamiliar with modern ERP systems, creating a substantial training challenge.

Assessing the Skill Gap

The HR department, in collaboration with the implementation team, conducted a comprehensive skill assessment across all departments. They identified several areas where training was critically needed:

1. Basic computer literacy for some non-technical staff
2. Understanding of ERP concepts and workflows
3. Specific Oracle Fusion module functionalities
4. Data analysis and reporting using Oracle Fusion tools

Comprehensive Training Program

To bridge the skill gap, a multi-tiered training program was developed:

1. **Foundational Training**: Basic computer and ERP concept training for staff who needed it.
2. **Role-Based Training**: Specialized training sessions focused on specific Oracle Fusion modules relevant to each department.
3. **Super User Program**: Intensive training for selected employees to become "Super Users" who could provide ongoing support to their colleagues.
4. **Continuous Learning**: Establishment of an online learning portal with video tutorials, user guides, and FAQs for ongoing reference.
5. **Hands-On Workshops**: Regular practical sessions where employees could practice using Oracle Fusion in a safe, test environment.

Budget and Resource Constraints

As with many large-scale projects, Al Shifa Hospital faced budget and resource constraints during the Oracle Fusion implementation. The project's scope and complexity led to unforeseen costs and resource requirements.

Financial Challenges

Several financial hurdles emerged during the implementation:

1. Unexpected hardware upgrades needed to support Oracle Fusion
2. Additional consulting hours required for complex integrations
3. Extended training costs due to the comprehensive nature of the system

Resource Allocation Issues

The hospital also faced challenges in allocating human resources to the project:

1. Key staff members were stretched thin between their regular duties and project responsibilities
2. Specialized skills, particularly in areas like data migration and API development, were in short supply

Strategies to Manage Constraints

To navigate these constraints, the project team employed several strategies:

1. **Prioritization**: The team worked with hospital leadership to prioritize features and modules, ensuring the most critical elements were implemented first.
2. **Flexible Staffing**: A combination of internal staff rotation and strategic use of external consultants helped balance the workload.
3. **Cloud Optimization**: Leveraging Oracle Fusion's cloud capabilities helped reduce hardware costs and IT maintenance burden.
4. **ROI Analysis**: Regular reviews of the project's return on investment helped justify additional funding when needed.
5. **Skills Development**: Investment in training internal staff for specialized roles reduced long-term dependence on external consultants.

Change Management Challenges

Implementing Oracle Fusion wasn't just a technical change; it represented a significant shift in how Al Shifa Hospital operated. Managing this organizational change proved to be one of the most complex challenges.

Identifying Change Management Issues

The implementation team identified several key areas where change management was crucial:

1. Altering long-established workflows and processes
2. Shifting responsibilities and job roles
3. Adapting to new performance metrics and reporting structures
4. Encouraging a data-driven decision-making culture

Comprehensive Change Management Strategy

To address these challenges, a robust change management strategy was developed:

1. **Leadership Alignment**: Ensuring all levels of leadership were aligned on the vision and actively supported the change.
2. **Stakeholder Analysis**: Identifying key stakeholders and their concerns, then tailoring communication and engagement strategies accordingly.
3. **Communication Plan**: Developing a clear, consistent communication plan that kept all staff informed about the progress, benefits, and upcoming changes.
4. **Process Redesign Workshops**: Involving staff in reimagining their workflows to leverage Oracle Fusion's capabilities fully.
5. **Feedback Mechanisms**: Establishing channels for employees to voice concerns and provide suggestions throughout the implementation process.
6. **Celebrating Milestones**: Recognizing and celebrating key achievements to maintain momentum and boost morale.

Performance and Scalability Issues

As Al Shifa Hospital began to implement Oracle Fusion, concerns arose about the system's performance and its ability to scale with the hospital's growth.

Identifying Performance Bottlenecks

During initial testing, several performance issues were identified:

1. Slow response times during peak usage hours
2. Long processing times for complex financial reports

3. Difficulties handling concurrent users during month-end closing processes

Ensuring Scalability

The team also needed to ensure that Oracle Fusion could accommodate Al Shifa's ambitious growth plans, including:

1. Opening new specialist clinics
2. Expanding bed capacity
3. Increasing outpatient services

Strategies for Optimizing Performance and Scalability

To address these challenges, the implementation team worked closely with Oracle consultants to develop solutions:

1. **Infrastructure Optimization**: Fine-tuning the cloud infrastructure to ensure optimal performance, including adjusting server configurations and network settings.
2. **Code Optimization**: Reviewing and optimizing custom code and integrations to improve efficiency.
3. **Load Testing**: Conducting extensive load testing to simulate peak usage scenarios and identify potential bottlenecks.
4. **Caching Strategies**: Implementing intelligent caching mechanisms to improve response times for frequently accessed data.
5. **Scalability Planning**: Designing the system architecture with scalability in mind, allowing for easy expansion as the hospital grows.
6. **Performance Monitoring**: Implementing robust monitoring tools to proactively identify and address performance issues.

Security and Compliance Challenges

Given the sensitive nature of healthcare data, ensuring the security and compliance of the new Oracle Fusion system was paramount. Al Shifa Hospital needed to navigate complex regulatory requirements while maintaining the highest standards of data protection.

Identifying Security Risks

The implementation team, in collaboration with the hospital's compliance officer, identified several key security concerns:

1. Data encryption for sensitive patient information
2. Access control and user authentication
3. Audit trails for all financial transactions
4. Compliance with healthcare data protection regulations

Regulatory Compliance Requirements

Al Shifa Hospital needed to ensure compliance with several regulations, including:

1. Local UAE healthcare data protection laws
2. International standards like HIPAA for potential international patients
3. Financial reporting standards for healthcare institutions

Strategies for Enhancing Security and Ensuring Compliance

To address these challenges, the team implemented a comprehensive security and compliance strategy:

1. **Multi-layered Security**: Implementing multiple layers of

security, including firewalls, intrusion detection systems, and advanced encryption protocols.

2. **Role-Based Access Control**: Developing a granular access control system based on job roles and responsibilities.
3. **Audit Trail Implementation**: Ensuring all system activities, especially those involving sensitive data or financial transactions, were logged and traceable.
4. **Regular Security Audits**: Establishing a schedule of regular security audits and penetration testing to identify and address vulnerabilities.
5. **Compliance Mapping**: Creating a detailed mapping of Oracle Fusion features to specific regulatory requirements to ensure full compliance.
6. **Data Anonymization**: Implementing data anonymization techniques for use in testing and training environments.
7. **Employee Training**: Conducting regular training sessions on data security best practices and compliance requirements.

User Adoption Challenges

Even with comprehensive training programs in place, ensuring widespread user adoption of Oracle Fusion proved to be an ongoing challenge. Some staff members struggled to embrace the new system fully, impacting the overall efficiency gains the hospital hoped to achieve.

Identifying Adoption Hurdles

Through user feedback and system usage analytics, several adoption challenges were identified:

1. Reluctance to abandon familiar workarounds and shadow systems

2. Difficulty in adapting to the new user interface
3. Lack of confidence in using advanced features
4. Inconsistent usage across departments

Strategies to Boost User Adoption

To address these challenges and encourage fuller adoption of Oracle Fusion, the implementation team developed several strategies:

1. **Personalized Support**: Offering one-on-one support sessions for users struggling with specific aspects of the system.
2. **Gamification**: Introducing elements of gamification, such as leaderboards and achievement badges, to encourage system exploration and usage.
3. **Success Stories**: Sharing success stories and case studies from departments or individuals who have effectively leveraged Oracle Fusion to improve their work.
4. **Continuous Improvement Workshops**: Organizing regular workshops where users could suggest improvements and learn about new features.
5. **User Groups**: Establishing user groups for different modules or departments to foster peer learning and support.
6. **Executive Sponsorship**: Enlisting hospital leadership to champion the use of Oracle Fusion and lead by example.

System Customization vs. Standardization Dilemma

As the implementation progressed, Al Shifa Hospital faced the classic dilemma of how much to customize Oracle Fusion to fit their existing processes versus adapting their processes to fit the system's standard functionality.

Balancing Act

The team needed to strike a delicate balance between:

1. Maintaining the benefits of a standardized, easily upgradable system
2. Ensuring the system met the unique needs of a UAE-based healthcare provider
3. Minimizing disruption to critical hospital operations

Strategies for Resolution

To navigate this challenge, the implementation team adopted several approaches:

1. **Process Evaluation**: Conducting a thorough evaluation of existing processes to determine which ones truly needed customization and which could be adapted to standard Oracle Fusion workflows.
2. **Customization Framework**: Developing a structured framework for evaluating and approving customization requests, considering factors like criticality, cost, and long-term maintainability.
3. **Configuration over Customization**: Leveraging Oracle Fusion's extensive configuration options to meet as many requirements as possible without resorting to customization.
4. **Phased Customization**: Implementing critical customizations in the initial phase, with plans to gradually reduce customizations in future updates as users adapt to the system.
5. **Best Practice Adoption**: Encouraging the adoption of industry best practices built into Oracle Fusion, even if they

required some process changes.

Integrating with External Systems

Al Shifa Hospital's operations extended beyond its walls, requiring integration with various external systems, including those of insurance providers, government health agencies, and partner healthcare facilities. Ensuring seamless integration with these external systems while maintaining data integrity and security posed a significant challenge.

Key Integration Points

The team identified several critical external integration points:

1. Insurance claim submission and processing systems
2. Government health information exchanges
3. Laboratory and diagnostic imaging systems from partner facilities
4. Pharmaceutical supply chain management systems

Strategies for Successful External Integration

To address the complexities of external system integration, the team employed several strategies:

1. **API-First Approach**: Adopting an API-first approach to integration, developing robust, well-documented APIs for external system connections.
2. **Data Standardization**: Implementing healthcare data standards like HL7 FHIR to ensure compatibility with a wide range of external systems.
3. **Secure Data Exchange**: Establishing secure data exchange

protocols, including encryption and secure file transfer methods.

4. **Automated Reconciliation**: Developing automated reconciliation processes to ensure data consistency between Oracle Fusion and external systems.
5. **Compliance Checks**: Implementing compliance checks within the integration processes to ensure all data exchanges met regulatory requirements.
6. **Scalable Integration Architecture**: Designing a scalable integration architecture that could easily accommodate new external systems as the hospital's network of partners grew.

Managing Stakeholder Expectations

Throughout the implementation process, managing the expectations of various stakeholders – from hospital leadership to frontline staff – proved to be an ongoing challenge. Different groups had varying ideas about what Oracle Fusion would deliver and how quickly benefits would be realized.

Identifying Stakeholder Groups

The team identified several key stakeholder groups, each with unique expectations:

1. Hospital Board and Executive Leadership
2. Department Heads and Middle Management
3. Finance and Accounting Teams
4. Clinical Staff (Doctors, Nurses, Technicians)
5. IT Department
6. Patients and Their Families

Strategies for Expectation Management

To effectively manage these diverse expectations, the implementation team developed a comprehensive stakeholder management plan:

1. **Expectation Mapping**: Conducting workshops with each stakeholder group to understand and document their expectations.
2. **Realistic Timeline Communication**: Clearly communicating realistic timelines for implementation phases and benefit realization.
3. **Regular Updates**: Providing regular, tailored updates to each stakeholder group on project progress and upcoming changes.
4. **Early Win Strategy**: Identifying and quickly implementing "quick wins" to demonstrate early value and maintain enthusiasm.
5. **Transparency about Challenges**: Being open about challenges faced and involving stakeholders in problem-solving where appropriate.
6. **Long-term Vision Alignment**: Continuously reinforcing how the Oracle Fusion implementation aligned with Al Shifa Hospital's long-term strategic vision.

Conclusion

The implementation of Oracle Fusion at Al Shifa Hospital was a journey fraught with challenges, from technical hurdles and resource constraints to change management issues and stakeholder expectations. However, through strategic planning, adaptability, and perseverance, the implementation team successfully navigated these obstacles.

Key to their success was a holistic approach that considered not just the technical aspects of the implementation but also the human and organizational factors. By addressing resistance to change, providing comprehensive training, ensuring robust security and compliance, and managing stakeholder expectations, Al Shifa Hospital was able to lay a strong foundation for the successful adoption of Oracle Fusion.

As the hospital moved forward with the implementation, the lessons learned from overcoming these challenges would prove invaluable. The experience gained would not only ensure the success of the Oracle Fusion project but also better prepare Al Shifa Hospital for future technological transformations in the ever-evolving healthcare landscape.

The journey of implementing Oracle Fusion demonstrated that with the right strategies, even the most complex challenges could be overcome, paving the way for a more efficient, data-driven, and financially robust healthcare institution.

Chapter 10 - Data Migration: Ensuring Accuracy and Completeness

Introduction

As Al Shifa Hospital embarked on its journey to implement Oracle Fusion Financials, one of the most critical and challenging aspects of the project emerged: data migration. The process of transferring existing financial data from legacy systems to the new Oracle Fusion platform was not merely a technical exercise but a fundamental step that would determine the success of the entire implementation. This chapter delves into the intricacies of the data migration process, highlighting the importance of data integrity, the challenges faced, and the strategies employed to ensure a smooth transition.

The Importance of Data Migration

Foundation for Future Success

Data migration serves as the foundation upon which the entire Oracle Fusion system would operate. Dr. Fatima Al-Mansoori, Al Shifa Hospital's CFO, understood this implicitly. "Our historical financial data is not just a record of our past," she explained to the project team. "It's the bedrock of our future financial decisions and analysis. We can't afford any mistakes in this process."

Ensuring Continuity of Operations

The hospital couldn't afford any disruption in its financial operations during the transition. Accurate and complete data migration was crucial to ensure that day-to-day financial activities, from patient billing to vendor payments, continued seamlessly.

Regulatory Compliance

In the highly regulated healthcare industry, maintaining accurate financial records is not just good practice—it's a legal requirement. The data migration process needed to ensure that all historical financial data remained compliant with local and international healthcare regulations.

Preparing for Data Migration

Forming the Data Migration Team

Recognizing the complexity of the task at hand, Al Shifa Hospital assembled a dedicated data migration team. This cross-functional group included:

- Financial experts from various departments
- IT specialists familiar with the existing systems
- Oracle Fusion consultants
- Data analysts
- Quality assurance professionals

Data Assessment and Inventory

The first task of the data migration team was to conduct a comprehensive assessment of the existing data. This involved:

1. Identifying all data sources: The team discovered that financial data was scattered across multiple systems, including:

- ○ The main accounting software
- ○ Separate systems for accounts receivable and payable
- ○ Excel spreadsheets used by different departments
- ○ Legacy systems from previously acquired clinics

2. Data volume analysis: The team estimated that they would need to migrate over 10 years of financial data, totaling approximately 50 million records.

3. Data quality evaluation: Initial assessments revealed varying levels of data quality across different systems. While the main accounting software maintained relatively clean data, some departmental spreadsheets contained inconsistencies and duplications.

Defining Data Migration Scope

With a clear understanding of the existing data landscape, the team worked with hospital leadership to define the scope of the data migration. Key decisions included:

- Migrating 10 years of historical data for comprehensive reporting and analysis
- Prioritizing critical financial data elements, such as general ledger transactions, patient billing records, and vendor payment history
- Identifying non-essential data that could be archived rather than migrated

Developing the Data Migration Strategy

Phased Approach

Given the volume and complexity of the data, the team opted for a phased migration approach:

1. Phase 1: Migration of master data (e.g., chart of accounts, vendor list, patient database)
2. Phase 2: Migration of historical transaction data
3. Phase 3: Migration of open transactions and balances

This approach allowed for better management of resources and more focused quality control at each stage.

Data Cleansing and Standardization

Before any data could be migrated, it needed to be cleansed and standardized. This process involved:

1. Removing duplicates: The team identified and eliminated duplicate records, particularly in patient and vendor databases.
2. Standardizing formats: Date formats, currency representations, and account codes were standardized across all data sources.
3. Filling data gaps: Missing information was identified and, where possible, populated through data enrichment processes.
4. Resolving inconsistencies: Discrepancies in financial records were investigated and resolved, often requiring collaboration with various department heads.

Mapping Data to Oracle Fusion

A critical step in the migration process was mapping the existing data structures to the Oracle Fusion data model. This involved:

1. Understanding the Oracle Fusion data structure
2. Creating detailed mapping documents for each data element
3. Identifying any custom fields or structures needed in Oracle Fusion to accommodate Al Shifa Hospital's specific requirements

Executing the Data Migration

Building and Testing Migration Scripts

With the strategy in place and data prepared, the technical team began developing migration scripts. These scripts were designed to:

1. Extract data from source systems
2. Transform the data according to the defined mappings
3. Load the data into Oracle Fusion

Each script underwent rigorous testing, first with small data samples and then with larger datasets. The team used a dedicated test environment to ensure that the scripts performed as expected without impacting the hospital's ongoing operations.

Dry Runs and Validation

Before the final migration, the team conducted several dry runs. These exercises served multiple purposes:

1. Identifying any performance issues with the migration scripts

2. Allowing for thorough validation of the migrated data
3. Providing opportunities for the team to refine and optimize the migration process

During these dry runs, financial experts meticulously checked the migrated data for accuracy and completeness. They focused on key areas such as:

- General ledger balances
- Patient account balances
- Vendor payment histories
- Fixed asset records

Any discrepancies were carefully documented and investigated, leading to further refinements in the migration scripts and processes.

Managing Data Cutover

As the go-live date approached, the team developed a detailed cutover plan. This plan outlined:

1. The sequence of migration activities
2. Specific roles and responsibilities during the cutover
3. Communication protocols
4. Contingency plans in case of unexpected issues

The actual data cutover was scheduled for a weekend to minimize disruption to hospital operations. Dr. Al-Mansoori and the hospital's CEO, Dr. Ahmed Al-Khalifa, were kept informed of progress throughout the cutover process.

Challenges and Solutions

Dealing with Legacy System Limitations

Challenge: Some of Al Shifa Hospital's older systems had limited export capabilities, making data extraction difficult.

Solution: The team developed custom extraction tools and, in some cases, manually extracted data from these systems. While time-consuming, this approach ensured that no critical data was left behind.

Handling Data Inconsistencies

Challenge: Inconsistencies in financial coding across different departments led to difficulties in data mapping.

Solution: The team worked closely with department heads to create a standardized coding system. This not only solved the immediate migration challenge but also improved financial reporting consistency for the future.

Managing Large Data Volumes

Challenge: The sheer volume of data, particularly in patient billing records, caused performance issues during initial migration attempts.

Solution: The team optimized the migration scripts and implemented a parallel processing approach. They also worked with the IT department to allocate additional server resources during the migration process.

Ensuring Data Privacy and Security

Challenge: Given the sensitive nature of patient financial data, ensuring data security throughout the migration process was paramount.

Solution: The team implemented stringent security measures, including data encryption during transfer, restricted access to migration environments, and comprehensive audit trails of all data handling activities.

Post-Migration Activities

Data Reconciliation

After the final data migration, a thorough reconciliation process was undertaken. This involved:

1. Comparing total balances in source systems with those in Oracle Fusion
2. Conducting detailed transaction-level reconciliations for critical accounts
3. Verifying the accuracy of migrated master data (e.g., vendor information, patient records)

User Verification

Key users from each department were involved in verifying the migrated data. They were tasked with:

1. Checking the accuracy of department-specific financial data
2. Verifying the availability and correctness of historical records
3. Ensuring that all necessary data elements were present for their day-to-day operations

Addressing Post-Migration Issues

Despite meticulous planning, some issues were inevitably discovered after the migration. The team established a rapid response process to address these issues, which included:

1. A dedicated helpdesk for users to report data discrepancies
2. Daily team meetings to prioritize and address reported issues
3. A process for making controlled adjustments to migrated data when necessary

Lessons Learned

The data migration process provided valuable insights that would benefit not only Al Shifa Hospital but also other organizations undertaking similar projects:

1. Early involvement of business users is crucial for understanding data nuances and ensuring accuracy.
2. Investing time in data cleansing and standardization pays dividends in smoother migration and improved data quality.
3. Multiple dry runs are essential for identifying and resolving issues before the final migration
4. Clear communication and expectation setting with hospital leadership and end-users help manage the challenges of the migration process.
5. Comprehensive documentation of the migration process, including decisions made and issues resolved, is invaluable for future reference and audits.

Impact on Al Shifa Hospital's Operations

The successful data migration laid a solid foundation for Al Shifa Hospital's use of Oracle Fusion Financials. Dr. Al-Mansoori noted several immediate benefits:

1. Improved data consistency across all financial processes
2. Enhanced ability to generate comprehensive financial reports spanning multiple years
3. Increased confidence in the accuracy of financial data for decision-making
4. Streamlined compliance processes due to better-organized and more accessible financial records

Conclusion

The data migration process, while challenging, proved to be a crucial step in Al Shifa Hospital's digital transformation journey. By ensuring the accuracy and completeness of their financial data in Oracle Fusion, the hospital positioned itself to leverage the full potential of the new system. As Dr. Al-Khalifa remarked, "The painstaking effort put into our data migration was like laying the foundation of a new building. It's not the most visible part, but it's absolutely essential for everything that follows."

As Al Shifa Hospital moved forward with its Oracle Fusion implementation, the solid data foundation would prove invaluable. The next critical phase would focus on another essential aspect of the project: user training and adoption. The success of the data migration set the stage for this next challenge, as users would now need to learn how to effectively utilize the wealth of accurate, migrated data within the new Oracle Fusion system.

Chapter 11 - User Training: Empowering Hospital Staff

Introduction

As Al Shifa Hospital approached the final stages of implementing Oracle Fusion Financials, the leadership team recognized that the success of this transformative project hinged on more than just cutting-edge technology. The true power of the new system would only be realized if the hospital staff could effectively leverage its capabilities. This chapter explores the comprehensive training program developed to empower Al Shifa's employees, ensuring they could harness the full potential of Oracle Fusion to drive financial excellence.

Assessing Training Needs

Identifying Key User Groups

The first step in developing an effective training program was to identify the various user groups within Al Shifa Hospital who would interact with Oracle Fusion. These groups included:

1. Finance department staff
2. Department managers and budget owners
3. Procurement team members
4. Human resources personnel
5. Executive leadership

Each group had unique needs and would use different aspects of the Oracle Fusion system. Understanding these distinctions was crucial for tailoring the training approach.

Skill Gap Analysis

To create targeted training modules, the implementation team conducted a thorough skill gap analysis. This process involved:

1. Surveying current staff competencies
2. Mapping required skills for each role in the new system
3. Identifying areas where additional training was needed

The results of this analysis provided valuable insights into the varying levels of technical proficiency among staff members and highlighted specific areas that required focused attention during the training process.

Developing a Comprehensive Training Strategy

Multi-tiered Approach

Based on the needs assessment, the training team developed a multi-tiered approach to cater to different user groups and skill levels:

1. Basic Oracle Fusion orientation for all staff
2. Role-specific training modules
3. Advanced sessions for power users and system administrators
4. Refresher courses and ongoing support

This stratified approach ensured that each employee received the appropriate level of training for their role while providing opportunities for those interested in deepening their expertise.

Blended Learning Methods

To accommodate different learning styles and maximize engagement, the training program incorporated a blend of learning methods:

1. Instructor-led classroom sessions
2. Interactive e-learning modules
3. Hands-on workshops
4. Self-paced tutorials
5. Job aids and quick reference guides

By offering a variety of learning formats, the program catered to the diverse needs of Al Shifa's staff, ensuring that everyone could find a method that suited their learning preferences.

Core Training Modules

Module 1: Oracle Fusion Fundamentals

This introductory module was designed to provide all staff members with a foundational understanding of Oracle Fusion. Topics covered included:

1. Overview of Oracle Fusion Financials
2. Navigation and user interface basics
3. System architecture and integration with other hospital systems
4. Security features and access controls
5. Basic troubleshooting and support channels

Module 2: General Ledger Essentials

Tailored for finance department staff and budget owners, this module focused on the General Ledger component of Oracle Fusion. Key areas of instruction included:

1. Chart of accounts structure and management
2. Journal entry creation and posting
3. Period close processes
4. Financial statement generation
5. Budgeting and forecasting tools

Module 3: Accounts Receivable and Patient Billing

This module was crucial for staff involved in patient billing and revenue cycle management. Topics covered were:

1. Patient account setup and management
2. Billing cycles and invoice generation
3. Payment processing and reconciliation
4. Collections management
5. Reporting and analytics for receivables

Module 4: Accounts Payable and Vendor Management

Designed for the procurement team and finance staff handling vendor payments, this module covered:

1. Vendor setup and maintenance
2. Purchase order processing
3. Invoice matching and approval workflows
4. Payment scheduling and execution
5. Vendor performance reporting

Module 5: Fixed Assets Management

This module was tailored for staff responsible for managing the hospital's equipment and infrastructure. Key topics included:

1. Asset registration and categorization
2. Depreciation methods and calculations
3. Asset maintenance scheduling
4. Disposal and transfer processes
5. Asset-related reporting and compliance

Module 6: Cash Management and Treasury

Focused on treasury staff and financial controllers, this module covered:

1. Bank account management
2. Cash position monitoring
3. Cash flow forecasting
4. Bank reconciliation processes
5. Investment and borrowing management

Module 7: Reporting and Analytics

This advanced module was designed for managers, executives, and analysts who needed to leverage Oracle Fusion's reporting capabilities:

1. Standard report customization
2. Ad-hoc query creation
3. Dashboard design and configuration
4. Data visualization techniques
5. Exporting and sharing reports

Specialized Training for System Administrators

Recognizing the critical role of system administrators in maintaining and optimizing Oracle Fusion, a dedicated training track was developed for this group. This intensive program covered:

1. System configuration and customization
2. User access management and security protocols
3. Data backup and recovery procedures
4. Performance monitoring and optimization
5. Integration management with other hospital systems
6. Troubleshooting complex issues

Training Delivery and Execution

Phased Roll-out

To minimize disruption to hospital operations, the training program was rolled out in phases:

1. Phase 1: Core finance team and system administrators
2. Phase 2: Department managers and budget owners
3. Phase 3: General staff and end-users

This approach allowed for the gradual build-up of in-house expertise, with early adopters supporting subsequent training phases.

Train-the-Trainer Model

To scale the training effort effectively, Al Shifa Hospital adopted a train-the-trainer model. Key staff members from each department were selected to become Oracle Fusion champions. These individuals received advanced training and were then responsible for:

1. Providing on-the-ground support to their colleagues
2. Conducting department-specific training sessions
3. Gathering feedback and identifying areas for additional training

This approach not only expanded the training capacity but also fostered a sense of ownership and expertise within each department.

Hands-on Learning Environment

To provide a safe space for staff to practice their new skills, a dedicated training environment was set up that mirrored the production system. This sandbox allowed users to:

1. Experiment with different scenarios without affecting live data
2. Practice complex processes multiple times
3. Explore advanced features without fear of making mistakes

The hands-on environment proved invaluable in building user confidence and proficiency.

Addressing Resistance and Encouraging Adoption

Change Management Strategies

Recognizing that implementing a new system can be met with resistance, the training program incorporated change management strategies to ease the transition:

1. Regular communication about the benefits of Oracle Fusion
2. Addressing concerns and misconceptions proactively
3. Celebrating early successes and quick wins

4. Providing channels for feedback and suggestions

Gamification and Incentives

To make the training process more engaging and encourage participation, gamification elements were introduced:

1. Skill badges for completing different training modules
2. Leaderboards showcasing top performers in training assessments
3. Recognition programs for staff who embraced and excelled in using Oracle Fusion

These elements added a fun, competitive aspect to the learning process and motivated staff to fully engage with the training program.

Post-Training Support and Continuous Learning

Help Desk and Support Channels

To ensure ongoing support after the initial training phase, Al Shifa Hospital established:

1. A dedicated Oracle Fusion help desk
2. An online knowledge base with FAQs and troubleshooting guides
3. A user forum for peer-to-peer support and knowledge sharing

These resources provided staff with multiple avenues to seek help and resolve issues quickly.

Refresher Courses and Advanced Training

Recognizing that learning is an ongoing process, the hospital implemented a program of continuous education:

1. Regular refresher courses on key modules
2. Advanced training sessions on new features and updates
3. Cross-training opportunities for staff interested in expanding their skills

This commitment to ongoing learning ensured that staff skills remained current and continued to evolve with the system.

Measuring Training Effectiveness

Key Performance Indicators (KPIs)

To assess the impact of the training program, several KPIs were established:

1. User proficiency scores in post-training assessments
2. Reduction in help desk tickets related to basic system usage
3. Increased efficiency in financial processes (e.g., faster month-end closes)
4. User satisfaction ratings with the Oracle Fusion system
5. Adoption rates of advanced features and reporting tools

Regular monitoring of these KPIs allowed the training team to identify areas of success and opportunities for improvement.

Feedback Loops and Continuous Improvement

The training program was designed to be dynamic and responsive to user needs. Feedback mechanisms included:

1. Post-training surveys
2. Focus group sessions with key user groups
3. Analysis of help desk trends and common issues

This feedback was used to continuously refine and improve the training materials and delivery methods.

Case Study: Finance Department Transformation

To illustrate the impact of the training program, let's examine the transformation within Al Shifa's finance department:

Before Oracle Fusion implementation, the finance team struggled with manual processes and disparate systems. The month-end close process typically took 15 days, with staff working long hours to reconcile accounts and generate reports.

After comprehensive Oracle Fusion training, the finance team experienced:

1. A reduction in month-end close time to just 5 days
2. 50% decrease in manual data entry errors
3. 30% increase in time spent on value-added analysis rather than data gathering
4. Improved collaboration with other departments through shared access to real-time financial data

Sarah, the Assistant Controller, remarked, "The training program didn't just teach us how to use Oracle Fusion; it showed us how to transform our entire approach to financial management. We're now able to provide much more timely and insightful financial guidance to hospital leadership."

Lessons Learned and Best Practices

As the training program progressed, several key lessons emerged:

1. Tailor training to specific roles and responsibilities
2. Provide ample hands-on practice opportunities
3. Leverage internal champions to drive adoption
4. Address the 'why' behind changes, not just the 'how'
5. Offer multiple learning formats to cater to different preferences
6. Maintain a continuous learning environment beyond initial implementation

These insights have become part of Al Shifa Hospital's best practices for any future system implementations or major upgrades.

Conclusion

The comprehensive user training program implemented at Al Shifa Hospital was a critical factor in the successful adoption of Oracle Fusion Financials. By empowering staff with the knowledge and skills to leverage the new system effectively, the hospital laid the foundation for a transformation in its financial operations.

As we move into the next chapter, we'll explore how this newly trained workforce began to integrate Oracle Fusion with other hospital systems, creating a seamless flow of information across departments and further enhancing operational efficiency.

Chapter 12 - System Integration: Connecting the Dots

Introduction: The Need for Seamless Information Flow

As Al Shifa Hospital embarked on its journey to implement Oracle Fusion Financials, it quickly became apparent that the success of this new system would heavily depend on its ability to integrate with existing hospital systems. In a modern healthcare environment, where patient care, administrative tasks, and financial management are all interconnected, the importance of smooth data flow between different departments cannot be overstated.

This chapter explores the intricate process of integrating Oracle Fusion with Al Shifa Hospital's existing systems, highlighting the challenges faced, solutions implemented, and the ultimate benefits realized. We'll delve into the technical aspects of system integration while also examining its impact on hospital operations and patient care.

Understanding the Integration Landscape

Existing Systems at Al Shifa Hospital

Before diving into the integration process, it's crucial to understand the complex ecosystem of systems already in place at Al Shifa Hospital. These included:

1. Electronic Health Record (EHR) System
2. Hospital Information System (HIS)
3. Laboratory Information System (LIS)
4. Picture Archiving and Communication System (PACS)
5. Pharmacy Management System
6. Human Resources Management System

7. Inventory Management System

Each of these systems played a vital role in the hospital's daily operations, storing and processing vast amounts of data. The challenge lay in ensuring that Oracle Fusion could seamlessly communicate with these existing systems, creating a unified and efficient information environment.

The Role of Oracle Fusion in the Integration Process

Oracle Fusion, with its modern architecture and robust integration capabilities, was well-positioned to serve as the central hub for Al Shifa Hospital's financial data. However, achieving this required careful planning and execution. The integration team, composed of Oracle consultants and Al Shifa's IT staff, identified several key objectives for the integration process:

1. Ensure real-time data synchronization between Oracle Fusion and other systems
2. Eliminate data silos and reduce manual data entry
3. Improve data accuracy and consistency across all systems
4. Enable comprehensive financial reporting and analytics
5. Enhance overall operational efficiency

With these objectives in mind, the team set out to create a detailed integration strategy.

Designing the Integration Architecture

Integration Patterns and Approaches

The integration team considered several integration patterns and approaches to connect Oracle Fusion with Al Shifa's existing systems.

After careful evaluation, they decided on a combination of the following:

1. **Point-to-Point Integration**: For systems requiring simple, direct connections with Oracle Fusion.
2. **Enterprise Service Bus (ESB)**: To facilitate more complex, multi-system integrations and enable future scalability.
3. **Web Services**: For real-time data exchange between systems using standard protocols.
4. **Batch Processing**: For large-scale data transfers that don't require real-time updates.

This multi-faceted approach allowed for flexibility in addressing the diverse integration needs of different systems while ensuring optimal performance and scalability.

Data Mapping and Transformation

One of the most critical aspects of the integration process was data mapping and transformation. This involved:

1. Identifying data elements in each system that needed to be shared
2. Defining the format and structure of data in each system
3. Creating mapping rules to transform data between systems
4. Establishing data validation and error handling processes

The team spent considerable time on this phase, working closely with department heads and system administrators to ensure that all necessary data points were accounted for and accurately mapped.

Integrating Oracle Fusion with Key Hospital Systems

Electronic Health Record (EHR) System Integration

The integration of Oracle Fusion with Al Shifa's EHR system was perhaps the most crucial aspect of the entire process. This integration aimed to streamline billing processes and improve financial tracking of patient care.

Key integration points included:

1. **Patient Registration**: Automatically creating financial records in Oracle Fusion when new patients are registered in the EHR system.
2. **Charge Capture**: Real-time transfer of billable items and services from the EHR to Oracle Fusion for accurate and timely invoicing.
3. **Insurance Verification**: Sharing insurance information between systems to facilitate claims processing.
4. **Payment Posting**: Updating patient accounts in both systems when payments are received.

The team implemented bi-directional web services to enable real-time data exchange between Oracle Fusion and the EHR system. This allowed for immediate updates to financial records as patient care was provided, significantly reducing billing errors and improving cash flow.

Hospital Information System (HIS) Integration

The integration with the Hospital Information System focused on synchronizing administrative and operational data with financial processes. Key integration points included:

1. **Bed Management**: Tracking occupied beds and associating them with patient accounts for accurate billing.
2. **Appointment Scheduling**: Linking scheduled procedures with financial pre-authorizations and cost estimates.
3. **Resource Allocation**: Connecting department-specific resource usage with cost center accounting in Oracle Fusion.

For this integration, the team utilized a combination of web services and batch processing. Real-time updates were implemented for critical data points, while less time-sensitive information was synchronized through nightly batch jobs.

Laboratory Information System (LIS) Integration

The integration of Oracle Fusion with the Laboratory Information System was crucial for accurate billing of laboratory tests and managing inventory of lab supplies. Key integration points included:

1. **Test Orders**: Automatic creation of billable items in Oracle Fusion when tests are ordered in the LIS.
2. **Results Reporting**: Linking test results with corresponding charges to ensure billing accuracy.
3. **Inventory Management**: Synchronizing lab supply usage with Oracle Fusion's inventory module for improved cost tracking and reordering.

The team implemented near real-time integration using web services, ensuring that financial records were updated promptly as laboratory services were rendered.

Pharmacy Management System Integration

Integrating Oracle Fusion with the Pharmacy Management System was essential for tracking medication costs and managing pharmaceutical inventory. Key integration points included:

1. **Medication Dispensing**: Real-time creation of charges in Oracle Fusion when medications are dispensed to patients.
2. **Inventory Control**: Synchronizing medication stock levels with Oracle Fusion's inventory module.
3. **Supplier Management**: Sharing supplier information between systems for streamlined procurement processes.

The integration team used a combination of web services and batch processing to handle the high volume of transactions generated by the pharmacy system while ensuring timely updates to financial records.

Human Resources Management System Integration

The integration of Oracle Fusion with Al Shifa's Human Resources Management System focused on aligning financial processes with workforce management. Key integration points included:

1. **Payroll Processing**: Synchronizing employee data and time records for accurate payroll calculation and posting.
2. **Benefits Administration**: Tracking benefit costs and employee contributions for comprehensive financial reporting.
3. **Position Control**: Linking staffing decisions with budgetary constraints and financial forecasting.

This integration primarily utilized batch processing, with nightly data synchronization between the two systems. However, critical updates, such as new hires or terminations, were processed in real-time to ensure immediate financial impact visibility.

Implementing Cross-System Workflows

One of the most significant benefits of integrating Oracle Fusion with Al Shifa's existing systems was the ability to create seamless, cross-system workflows. These workflows automated complex processes that previously required manual intervention and data entry across multiple systems.

Patient Admission to Discharge Workflow

The team implemented an end-to-end workflow that tracked a patient's journey from admission to discharge, encompassing clinical, administrative, and financial processes. This workflow included:

1. Patient registration in the EHR system, automatically creating a financial account in Oracle Fusion
2. Real-time updates to the financial account as services are rendered and recorded in various clinical systems
3. Automatic generation of insurance claims based on clinical documentation
4. Tracking of payments and adjustments across systems
5. Final bill generation and financial closure upon patient discharge

This integrated workflow significantly reduced manual data entry, minimized billing errors, and improved the overall patient experience by streamlining administrative processes.

Procurement to Payment Workflow

Another crucial workflow implemented was the procurement to payment process, which spanned multiple systems:

1. Requisition creation in the Inventory Management System
2. Approval routing through Oracle Fusion based on predefined rules
3. Purchase order generation and transmission to suppliers
4. Goods receipt recording in the Inventory Management System
5. Invoice matching and payment processing in Oracle Fusion

This integrated workflow improved procurement efficiency, enhanced financial control, and provided real-time visibility into the hospital's purchasing activities and liabilities.

Ensuring Data Quality and Consistency

With data flowing between multiple systems, maintaining data quality and consistency became paramount. The integration team implemented several measures to address this challenge:

Data Validation Rules

Robust data validation rules were implemented at various integration points to ensure that only clean, properly formatted data was transferred between systems. These rules included:

1. Format checks (e.g., date formats, numeric values)
2. Range validations (e.g., acceptable values for specific fields)
3. Relationship checks (e.g., ensuring patient IDs exist in both systems)

4. Completeness checks (e.g., all required fields are populated)

Any data failing these validation checks was flagged for review and correction before being processed further.

Master Data Management

To maintain consistency across systems, the team implemented a master data management (MDM) approach for key data elements such as:

1. Patient demographics
2. Provider information
3. Insurance plans
4. Service codes and charge masters

The MDM solution ensured that these critical data elements were synchronized across all integrated systems, reducing discrepancies and improving overall data quality.

Audit Trails and Error Logging

Comprehensive audit trails and error logging mechanisms were put in place to track data movements and identify integration issues. This included:

1. Logging all data transfers between systems
2. Recording any data validation failures or processing errors
3. Implementing alerts for critical integration failures
4. Creating dashboards for monitoring integration health and performance

These measures allowed the IT team to quickly identify and resolve any integration issues, minimizing disruptions to hospital operations.

Security and Compliance Considerations

Integrating multiple systems inevitably raises concerns about data security and regulatory compliance. The integration team worked closely with Al Shifa's compliance officer to ensure that the integrated environment met all necessary security and privacy requirements.

Data Encryption and Access Control

All data transfers between Oracle Fusion and other systems were encrypted using industry-standard protocols. Additionally, robust access control measures were implemented to ensure that users could only access data relevant to their roles across the integrated systems.

Audit and Compliance Reporting

The integrated environment was designed to facilitate comprehensive audit and compliance reporting. This included:

1. Tracking all data access and modifications across systems
2. Generating audit reports for regulatory compliance (e.g., HIPAA)
3. Implementing data retention and archiving policies across all integrated systems

These measures ensured that Al Shifa Hospital could maintain compliance with healthcare regulations while benefiting from the improved efficiency of the integrated systems.

Performance Optimization and Scalability

As the integration between Oracle Fusion and Al Shifa's existing systems went live, the team focused on optimizing performance and ensuring scalability for future growth.

Performance Monitoring and Tuning

The team implemented comprehensive performance monitoring tools to track:

1. Response times for real-time integrations
2. Processing times for batch jobs
3. System resource utilization during peak integration periods

Based on these metrics, the team continuously fine-tuned the integration processes, optimizing database queries, adjusting batch job schedules, and balancing server loads to ensure optimal performance.

Scalability Planning

Anticipating Al Shifa Hospital's future growth, the integration architecture was designed with scalability in mind. This included:

1. Implementing a modular integration approach that allows for easy addition of new systems
2. Utilizing cloud-based integration services for improved flexibility and scalability
3. Designing integration processes to handle increasing data volumes without significant performance degradation

These measures ensured that the integrated environment could grow and evolve alongside Al Shifa Hospital's expanding operations.

Training and Change Management

The successful integration of Oracle Fusion with existing systems was not just a technical challenge but also a significant change for Al Shifa's staff. The team recognized the importance of comprehensive training and change management to ensure smooth adoption of the new integrated environment.

Cross-System Training Programs

The team developed and delivered training programs that focused not just on individual systems but on the end-to-end processes that now spanned multiple systems. This included:

1. Overview sessions on the integrated environment and its benefits
2. Hands-on training for new cross-system workflows
3. Guidance on troubleshooting common integration issues

These training programs helped staff understand the big picture and appreciate how their actions in one system could impact processes in another.

Change Management Initiatives

To facilitate smooth adoption of the integrated systems, the team implemented several change management initiatives:

1. Regular communication about integration milestones and benefits
2. Appointment of "Integration Champions" in each department to provide peer support
3. Feedback mechanisms for staff to report issues or suggest

improvements
4. Gradual rollout of new integrated processes to allow for adjustment periods

These initiatives helped build staff confidence in the new integrated environment and minimized resistance to change.

Measuring Integration Success

As the integrated environment stabilized, the team focused on measuring the success of the integration efforts. Key performance indicators (KPIs) were established to track the impact of integration on hospital operations and financial performance.

Operational Efficiency Metrics

The team tracked several metrics to assess improvements in operational efficiency:

1. Reduction in manual data entry time
2. Decrease in billing errors and claim rejections
3. Improvement in cash flow and accounts receivable days
4. Reduction in time spent on reconciliation between systems

Initial results showed significant improvements across all these metrics, with manual data entry time reduced by 60% and billing errors decreased by 40%.

Financial Impact Assessment

The financial impact of the integration was measured through:

1. Improved revenue capture due to more accurate and timely

billing
2. Cost savings from reduced administrative overhead
3. Better financial forecasting capabilities due to real-time data availability
4. Enhanced ability to identify and address revenue leakage

Early assessments indicated that the integration efforts had contributed to a 15% improvement in revenue capture and a 10% reduction in administrative costs.

User Satisfaction Surveys

The team conducted regular surveys to gauge user satisfaction with the integrated environment. These surveys measured:

1. Ease of use of cross-system workflows
2. Perceived improvement in job efficiency
3. Confidence in data accuracy and consistency
4. Overall satisfaction with the integrated systems

Initial survey results showed high levels of user satisfaction, with 85% of staff reporting improved job efficiency and 90% expressing confidence in data accuracy.

Continuous Improvement and Future Roadmap

With the core integration between Oracle Fusion and Al Shifa's existing systems in place, the team shifted focus to continuous improvement and planning for future enhancements.

Ongoing Optimization Efforts

The team established a process for ongoing optimization of the integrated environment, including:

1. Regular review of integration performance metrics
2. Solicitation of user feedback on integration pain points
3. Continuous refinement of data mapping and transformation rules
4. Periodic reassessment of integration architecture to incorporate new technologies

These efforts ensured that the integrated environment continued to evolve and improve over time.

Future Integration Initiatives

Looking ahead, the team identified several areas for future integration enhancements:

1. Implementing advanced analytics capabilities across the integrated data set
2. Exploring AI and machine learning opportunities for predictive financial modeling
3. Integrating with external healthcare networks for improved care coordination and financial management
4. Implementing blockchain technology for secure, distributed patient records and financial transactions

These future initiatives promised to further leverage the integrated environment to drive innovation and improve patient care at Al Shifa Hospital.

Conclusion: The Power of Connected Systems

The integration of Oracle Fusion with Al Shifa Hospital's existing systems marked a significant milestone in the hospital's digital transformation journey. By creating a seamless flow of information across clinical, administrative, and financial systems, Al Shifa was able to achieve new levels of operational efficiency, financial accuracy, and data-driven decision-making.

The success of this integration effort demonstrated the power of connected systems in a modern healthcare environment. It showed that when implemented thoughtfully and with a focus on both technical and human factors, system integration can be a powerful driver of organizational improvement.

As Al Shifa Hospital continues to build on this integrated foundation, it is well-positioned to meet the evolving challenges of healthcare delivery and financial management. The connected systems not only improve the hospital's bottom line but also contribute to its ultimate goal: providing exceptional patient care in an efficient and sustainable manner.

Chapter 13 - Customization and Configuration: Tailoring to Al Shifa's Needs

Introduction

As the implementation of Oracle Fusion at Al Shifa Hospital progressed, it became increasingly clear that the out-of-the-box solution, while powerful, would need significant customization to fully meet the unique needs of the healthcare institution. This chapter explores the intricate process of adapting Oracle Fusion to align with Al Shifa's specific requirements, workflows, and organizational structure. We'll delve into the challenges faced, the strategies employed, and the outcomes achieved through this crucial phase of the implementation journey.

Assessing Al Shifa's Unique Requirements

Identifying Hospital-Specific Processes

The first step in tailoring Oracle Fusion to Al Shifa's needs was a comprehensive assessment of the hospital's existing processes and requirements. The implementation team, led by the hospital's CFO, Sarah Al-Mansoori, worked closely with department heads to identify areas where standard Oracle Fusion functionality might fall short.

One key area of focus was the hospital's complex billing structure, which varied depending on the type of patient (insured, self-pay, government-sponsored) and the nature of the medical services provided. The team realized that the standard Accounts Receivable module would need significant customization to accommodate these nuances.

Regulatory Compliance Considerations

Another critical factor in the customization process was ensuring compliance with local healthcare regulations and reporting requirements. The UAE's healthcare sector is heavily regulated, with strict guidelines on financial reporting, patient data privacy, and insurance claim processing. The implementation team had to carefully review these regulations and design customizations that would enable Al Shifa to meet its compliance obligations seamlessly.

Customization Strategies

Extending Standard Functionality

With a clear understanding of Al Shifa's unique requirements, the implementation team began the process of extending Oracle Fusion's standard functionality. This involved leveraging Oracle's powerful customization tools to create new fields, workflows, and business rules without altering the core system code.

For example, to address the complex billing structure, the team extended the Accounts Receivable module to include additional fields for patient type and service category. They also created custom pricing rules that automatically applied the correct rates based on these factors.

Developing Custom Reports

Reporting was another area that required significant customization. While Oracle Fusion comes with a robust set of standard reports, many of these did not align with Al Shifa's specific reporting needs or regulatory requirements. The implementation team worked with the hospital's finance department to design and develop a suite of custom reports that provided the exact information needed for internal decision-making and external compliance.

One particularly challenging report was the monthly financial performance dashboard requested by the hospital board. This required pulling data from multiple Oracle Fusion modules and presenting it in a visually appealing and easily digestible format. The team used Oracle's Business Intelligence Publisher tool to create this complex report, which became a critical tool for hospital leadership.

Integrating with Existing Systems

Al Shifa Hospital had several legacy systems that needed to integrate with Oracle Fusion. These included the hospital's electronic health record (EHR) system, the human resources management system, and the inventory management system for medical supplies.

Integrating these systems with Oracle Fusion required careful planning and execution. The team used Oracle's integration tools to create seamless data flows between the systems. For instance, they set up a real-time integration between the EHR system and Oracle Fusion's Accounts Receivable module, ensuring that billing information was always up-to-date and accurate.

Configuration Challenges

Chart of Accounts Structure

One of the most significant configuration challenges was designing a chart of accounts structure that met Al Shifa's reporting needs while also aligning with Oracle Fusion's best practices. The hospital's existing chart of accounts was complex and hierarchical, reflecting the various departments, cost centers, and funding sources.

The implementation team worked closely with Al Shifa's finance department to redesign the chart of accounts. They leveraged Oracle Fusion's flexible account structure to create a streamlined yet comprehensive chart of accounts that supported both detailed departmental reporting and high-level financial analysis.

Security and Access Control

Given the sensitive nature of financial and patient data, configuring appropriate security and access controls was a critical task. The team had to balance the need for data protection with the requirement for efficient workflows and collaboration across departments.

They utilized Oracle Fusion's role-based access control features to create a granular security model. This involved defining specific roles for different job functions within the hospital and assigning appropriate permissions to each role. For example, nurses in the billing department were given access to enter charges but not to adjust or write off balances, while finance managers had full access to financial reports and adjustment capabilities.

Workflow Configuration

Configuring workflows to match Al Shifa's approval processes and operational procedures was another significant challenge. The hospital had complex approval hierarchies for various financial transactions, from purchase orders to journal entries.

The team used Oracle Fusion's workflow builder to create custom approval flows that mirrored Al Shifa's existing processes. They also implemented automated notifications and reminders to ensure that approvals were processed in a timely manner, improving overall operational efficiency.

User Experience Enhancements

Customizing the User Interface

To improve user adoption and efficiency, the implementation team focused on customizing the Oracle Fusion user interface to make it more intuitive for Al Shifa's staff. This involved reorganizing menu structures, creating custom dashboards, and designing simplified data entry forms for common tasks.

For instance, they created a custom "Patient Billing" dashboard that brought together all the relevant information and actions needed by the billing staff, reducing the need to navigate between multiple screens and improving productivity.

Mobile Access Configuration

Recognizing the need for on-the-go access to financial information, the team configured Oracle Fusion's mobile capabilities to allow key personnel to access reports and approve transactions from their smartphones or tablets. This was particularly valuable for department heads and executives who were often away from their desks but needed to stay informed and make timely decisions.

Testing and Validation

User Acceptance Testing

As customizations and configurations were implemented, rigorous testing was essential to ensure that the system met Al Shifa's requirements and functioned as intended. The team organized extensive user acceptance testing (UAT) sessions, involving staff from various departments to validate the customizations.

During these sessions, users were asked to perform their day-to-day tasks in the customized Oracle Fusion environment and provide feedback. This process uncovered several issues that required further refinement, such as the need for additional fields in certain data entry forms and adjustments to workflow approvals.

Performance Testing

Given the scale of customizations implemented, it was crucial to ensure that system performance was not negatively impacted. The team conducted thorough performance testing, simulating high-volume scenarios to verify that the system could handle Al Shifa's peak workloads without significant slowdowns.

This testing revealed some performance bottlenecks, particularly in custom reports that were pulling large amounts of data. The team optimized these reports, implementing caching strategies and refining database queries to improve response times.

Change Management and Training

Communicating Customizations

As the customized Oracle Fusion system took shape, effective communication with end-users became increasingly important. The implementation team developed a comprehensive communication plan to keep all stakeholders informed about the changes and how they would impact daily operations.

They created detailed documentation outlining the customizations and new features, distributed regular updates via email and the hospital's intranet, and held town hall meetings to address questions and concerns from staff.

Tailored Training Programs

The customizations and configurations necessitated a tailored training program for Al Shifa's staff. The team developed role-specific training modules that focused on the customized aspects of the system relevant to each job function.

For example, billing staff received in-depth training on the new custom fields and workflows in the Accounts Receivable module, while finance managers were trained on using the new custom reports and dashboards for financial analysis.

Continuous Improvement

Feedback Loops

Recognizing that the customization process doesn't end with the initial implementation, the team established feedback loops to continuously gather input from users and identify areas for further improvement. They set up a dedicated email address for system feedback and regularly conducted user surveys to assess satisfaction with the customized Oracle Fusion system.

Iterative Refinement

Based on the feedback received, the team implemented an iterative refinement process. They prioritized user requests and system enhancements, implementing them in regular update cycles. This approach ensured that the Oracle Fusion system continued to evolve and improve, aligning ever more closely with Al Shifa's changing needs.

Measuring Success

Key Performance Indicators

To gauge the success of the customization and configuration efforts, the team established a set of key performance indicators (KPIs). These included metrics such as user adoption rates, system response times, reduction in manual data entry, and improvements in financial reporting accuracy and timeliness.

ROI Assessment

The team also conducted a preliminary return on investment (ROI) assessment to quantify the benefits of the customizations. This involved comparing the costs of customization against the operational efficiencies gained and the improved decision-making capabilities enabled by the tailored system.

Early results were promising, showing significant time savings in key processes such as month-end closing and financial reporting. The custom dashboards and mobile access features were particularly well-received, with hospital leadership reporting improved visibility into financial performance and faster decision-making.

Lessons Learned

Balancing Customization and Standard Functionality

One of the key lessons learned during this phase was the importance of striking the right balance between customization and leveraging standard Oracle Fusion functionality. While customizations were necessary to meet Al Shifa's unique needs, the team found that over-customization could lead to increased complexity and potential issues with future system upgrades.

They adopted a "customize only when necessary" approach, carefully evaluating each customization request to determine if it could be addressed through configuration of standard features or if true customization was required.

Importance of User Involvement

Another crucial lesson was the value of involving end-users throughout the customization process. By engaging users early and often, the team was able to ensure that customizations truly met the needs of those who would be using the system daily. This user-centric approach not only resulted in more effective customizations but also improved user buy-in and adoption of the new system.

Documentation and Knowledge Transfer

The team also learned the critical importance of thorough documentation and knowledge transfer. As customizations were implemented, they made sure to document not only the technical details but also the business rationale behind each change. This documentation proved invaluable for training, troubleshooting, and future system maintenance.

Conclusion

The process of customizing and configuring Oracle Fusion to meet Al Shifa Hospital's unique needs was complex and challenging, but ultimately rewarding. Through careful assessment, strategic customization, and thoughtful configuration, the implementation team was able to transform Oracle Fusion from a powerful but generic financial management system into a tailored solution that aligned closely with Al Shifa's specific requirements and workflows.

The success of this phase laid a strong foundation for the subsequent stages of the implementation, setting the stage for a smooth transition to the new system and positioning Al Shifa Hospital to realize significant benefits from its investment in Oracle Fusion. As we move into the next chapter, we'll explore the exciting and tense moments as Al Shifa Hospital prepares for and executes the big switch to their newly customized Oracle Fusion system.

Chapter 14 - Going Live: The Big Switch

The Calm Before the Storm

As the sun rose over Dubai's skyline, casting a golden glow on Al Shifa Hospital's gleaming facade, an air of anticipation filled the corridors. Today was the day - the culmination of months of meticulous planning, tireless effort, and unwavering dedication. The hospital was about to make the monumental switch to Oracle Fusion, a transition that promised to revolutionize its financial operations.

Dr. Amira Hassan, the hospital's CEO, stood at the window of her office, her usual composed demeanor tinged with a hint of nervous energy. She recalled the journey that had led them to this pivotal moment - the financial challenges that had once threatened the hospital's future, the decision to implement Oracle Fusion, and the countless hours spent preparing for this day.

Final Preparations

Last-Minute Checks

In the IT department, Farid Khalil, the Chief Information Officer, and his team were conducting final system checks. Rows of computer screens flickered with activity as they ran through their pre-launch checklist one last time.

"All modules are green," announced Sarah, the lead systems analyst. "General Ledger, Accounts Receivable, Accounts Payable, Fixed Assets, and Cash Management - all systems are go."

Farid nodded, his eyes never leaving the main monitor. "Excellent. Let's run the integration test one more time. We can't afford any surprises once we flip the switch."

Training Reinforcement

Meanwhile, in the hospital's main auditorium, Layla Mansour, the Head of Training, was conducting a last-minute refresher session for key staff members. The room buzzed with a mix of excitement and apprehension as employees from various departments gathered to review the new processes.

"Remember," Layla emphasized, her voice carrying across the room, "the principles we've learned over the past months remain the same. The Oracle Fusion interface might look different, but the core financial concepts haven't changed. Trust your training, and don't hesitate to reach out to your designated support personnel if you need assistance."

Command Center Setup

In a large conference room that had been transformed into a command center, Hassan Ali, the project manager from Oracle, was briefing his team of consultants. Whiteboards covered with flowcharts and contingency plans lined the walls, and a bank of computers had been set up to monitor every aspect of the go-live process.

"We've prepared for this moment for months," Hassan said, his voice steady and confident. "Each of you knows your role. Remember, clear communication is key. Any issues, no matter how small, need to be reported and logged immediately."

The Moment of Truth

The Countdown Begins

As the clock ticked closer to the designated launch time, key personnel gathered in the command center. Dr. Amira Hassan stood at the head of the room, flanked by Farid Khalil and Omar Nasser, the hospital's CFO.

"Ladies and gentlemen," Dr. Hassan began, her voice carrying a mix of gravity and optimism, "we stand at the threshold of a new era for Al Shifa Hospital. The implementation of Oracle Fusion represents not just a technological upgrade, but a fundamental shift in how we manage our finances and, by extension, how we care for our patients."

She paused, looking around the room at the faces of those who had worked tirelessly to bring this moment to fruition. "I want to thank each and every one of you for your dedication, your expertise, and your belief in this project. Now, let's make history."

Flipping the Switch

With a nod from Dr. Hassan, Farid stepped forward. His hand hovered over the keyboard, poised to enter the command that would initiate the switch to Oracle Fusion.

"Systems check?" he asked, his voice steady despite the tension in the room.

"All systems ready," came the response from his team.

"Database backup confirmed," added another voice.

"Support teams on standby," reported Layla.

Farid took a deep breath. "On my mark. Three... two... one... execute."

With a final keystroke, the command was given. For a moment, the room fell silent, the only sound the soft hum of computers and the collective held breath of everyone present.

Then, one by one, the monitors came to life. Graphs and charts flickered into existence, data streams began to flow, and the Oracle Fusion dashboard materialized on the main screen.

"Initial diagnostics show all systems functioning normally," announced Sarah, her voice tinged with relief and excitement.

A collective sigh of relief swept through the room, followed by a smattering of applause. But the tension wasn't fully broken - everyone knew that the real test was yet to come.

The First Hours

Monitoring and Rapid Response

As the new system came online, the command center burst into action. Teams of analysts hunched over their stations, monitoring every aspect of the transition. The room buzzed with activity as data flows were checked, user logins were verified, and the first transactions began to process through the new system.

"We're seeing a slight lag in the Accounts Receivable module," called out one of the Oracle consultants. "Investigating now."

Farid and his team quickly huddled around the consultant's station, diving deep into the code to identify and resolve the issue. Within minutes, they had isolated the problem - a minor configuration error - and implemented a fix.

"AR module now operating at optimal speed," the consultant confirmed, eliciting a round of thumbs-up from the team.

Early Challenges

As the morning progressed, the inevitable teething problems began to surface. In the hospital's billing department, a staff member reported difficulty accessing patient payment histories.

"I can see the current balance, but I can't view the transaction details," she explained over the phone to the support team.

The issue was quickly escalated to the command center, where it was discovered that a permissions setting had been overlooked during the user role configuration. A rapid fix was deployed, resolving the issue not just for the reporting staff member, but for all users in similar roles.

In the pharmacy, another challenge arose. The integration between Oracle Fusion and the inventory management system was showing discrepancies in stock levels.

"We're showing negative quantities for some high-turnover items," the head pharmacist reported, a note of concern in his voice.

This issue required a more complex solution, involving both the Oracle Fusion team and the inventory system vendors. Over a tense hour, they worked to reconcile the data discrepancies and adjust the integration parameters to ensure accurate stock reporting.

User Experiences

Adapting to Change

As the day wore on, the hospital staff began to adapt to the new system. In the finance department, Aisha, a senior accountant, found herself navigating the Oracle Fusion interface with increasing confidence.

"It's different, but in a good way," she remarked to a colleague. "Once you get used to the layout, you can see how much more efficient it is. I've already closed three month-end reports in the time it used to take me to do one!"

Not all experiences were as smooth, however. In the human resources department, Khalid, a payroll specialist, was struggling with the new process for inputting overtime hours.

"I can't seem to find the right field," he muttered, frustration evident in his voice. "It was so much simpler in the old system."

A nearby support staff member, overhearing his complaint, quickly came to his aid. After a brief tutorial, Khalid's frown transformed into a smile of understanding.

"Oh, I see now," he said, nodding. "It actually makes more sense this way. It'll just take some getting used to."

Real-Time Insights

In the executive offices, Omar Nasser, the CFO, was exploring the new real-time reporting capabilities of Oracle Fusion. His eyes widened as he pulled up a dynamic cash flow forecast that adjusted in real-time as new data entered the system.

"This is incredible," he murmured, already seeing the potential for more informed decision-making. "We've never had this level of visibility before."

The First Day Winds Down

Evening Assessment

As the sun began to set, casting long shadows across the hospital grounds, the command center remained a hive of activity. Dr. Hassan reconvened the key stakeholders for an evening assessment of the day's events.

"Status report," she requested, looking to Farid and the Oracle team.

Farid stepped forward, tablet in hand. "Overall, the transition has been successful," he began. "We've encountered several minor issues and two significant challenges, all of which have been resolved. System performance is stable, and we're seeing positive feedback from many departments."

Hassan Ali, the Oracle project manager, added his perspective. "From our standpoint, this has been a remarkably smooth go-live. The preparation and training have really paid off. We're seeing user adoption rates well above average for a project of this scale."

Omar Nasser, the CFO, couldn't contain his enthusiasm. "The financial insights we're already gaining are extraordinary," he reported. "We're seeing patterns and trends that were previously hidden or would have taken weeks to uncover."

Dr. Hassan nodded, a smile of relief and pride crossing her face. "Excellent work, everyone. But let's not get complacent. What's our plan for ongoing monitoring and support?"

The Path Forward

Layla Mansour, the Head of Training, outlined the support strategy. "We have support staff stationed in every department, working in shifts to provide 24/7 coverage. We've also set up a dedicated helpline and an online knowledge base for user queries."

Farid chimed in, "My team will be monitoring system performance round the clock for the next week. We've set up alerts for any anomalies, and we have rapid response protocols in place."

"Additionally," added Hassan Ali, "we have a team of Oracle experts on standby, ready to assist with any complex issues that may arise."

Dr. Hassan took in the information, her expression one of cautious optimism. "It sounds like we're well-prepared. Now, let's discuss our priorities for the coming days..."

Reflections and Looking Ahead

As the meeting concluded and the team prepared for the challenges of the coming days, there was a palpable sense of accomplishment in the air. The big switch - the moment they had all been working towards for so long - had finally happened.

Dr. Hassan lingered in the command center after the others had left, gazing at the screens that now displayed the heartbeat of Al Shifa Hospital's new financial nervous system. She reflected on the journey that had brought them here - the initial struggles, the decision to embrace change, the hard work and dedication of every team member.

The implementation of Oracle Fusion was more than just a technology upgrade; it represented a fundamental shift in how Al Shifa Hospital would operate. It promised greater efficiency, better financial control, and ultimately, improved patient care.

As she turned to leave, Dr. Hassan allowed herself a moment of pride. They had taken a leap into the future, and while challenges undoubtedly lay ahead, she was confident that they were now better equipped than ever to face them.

The big switch was just the beginning. The real transformation of Al Shifa Hospital was only just beginning to unfold.

Chapter 15 - Early Wins: Immediate Benefits Realized

Introduction

As the dust settled from the monumental "Go Live" event at Al Shifa Hospital, the anticipation and nervous energy that had permeated the corridors began to give way to a sense of excitement and accomplishment. The implementation of Oracle Fusion Financials was no small feat, and the entire organization had invested significant time, resources, and effort into making this transition a success. Now, in the wake of this transformative change, it was time to take stock of the immediate benefits and early wins that the new system had brought to the hospital's financial operations.

This chapter will explore the tangible improvements and positive outcomes observed in the first few months following the Oracle Fusion implementation. We'll delve into various aspects of the hospital's financial processes, examining how the new system has streamlined operations, enhanced accuracy, and provided valuable insights to decision-makers. By highlighting these early wins, we aim to demonstrate the immediate value that Oracle Fusion has brought to Al Shifa Hospital and set the stage for long-term success.

Improved Financial Visibility

One of the most significant and immediate benefits realized by Al Shifa Hospital was the dramatic improvement in financial visibility across the organization. The Oracle Fusion system provided a centralized platform for all financial data, offering real-time insights into the hospital's financial health.

Real-Time Reporting

Prior to the implementation of Oracle Fusion, generating comprehensive financial reports was a time-consuming process that often involved manual data consolidation from various departments. With the new system in place, Al Shifa's finance team could now access up-to-the-minute financial information with just a few clicks.

Dr. Fatima Al-Mahmoud, the hospital's CFO, remarked, "The speed at which we can now generate accurate financial reports is truly remarkable. What used to take days or even weeks can now be accomplished in minutes. This real-time visibility allows us to make informed decisions quickly and respond to financial challenges proactively."

Enhanced Dashboard Functionality

Oracle Fusion's intuitive dashboards provided hospital leadership with a bird's-eye view of key financial metrics. These customizable dashboards allowed executives to monitor critical performance indicators such as cash flow, accounts receivable aging, and department-specific budgets at a glance.

Ahmed Hassan, the CEO of Al Shifa Hospital, shared his experience: "The executive dashboards have transformed the way we approach our weekly leadership meetings. Instead of poring over static reports, we now have dynamic, real-time data at our fingertips. This allows us to focus our discussions on strategic decision-making rather than simply reviewing historical information."

Drill-Down Capabilities

Another early win for the finance team was the ability to drill down into specific transactions from high-level reports. This feature allowed for quick investigation of any discrepancies or anomalies, significantly reducing the time spent on financial inquiries and audits.

Laila Khalid, a senior accountant at Al Shifa, noted, "The drill-down functionality has been a game-changer for our team. We can now trace the origin of any financial entry within seconds, which has greatly improved our ability to respond to inquiries from department heads and external auditors."

Streamlined Financial Close Process

One of the most immediate and impactful benefits of the Oracle Fusion implementation was the dramatic improvement in the monthly and quarterly financial close processes. The hospital's finance team experienced a significant reduction in the time and effort required to complete these critical tasks.

Automated Reconciliations

Oracle Fusion's automated reconciliation features eliminated much of the manual work previously required to balance accounts at the end of each period. The system automatically matched transactions across different modules, flagging discrepancies for review and significantly reducing the potential for human error.

Nasser Al-Qasimi, the head of the reconciliation team, shared his observations: "In our first month-end close with Oracle Fusion, we saw a 40% reduction in the time spent on reconciliations. The automated matching process caught several discrepancies that might have been overlooked in our old manual process, improving the accuracy of our financial statements."

Standardized Close Checklist

The implementation team worked closely with Al Shifa's finance department to create a standardized close checklist within Oracle Fusion. This digital checklist ensured that all necessary steps were completed in the correct order and provided real-time visibility into the progress of the close process.

Amira Saeed, the financial controller, commented on the impact of this feature: "The standardized close checklist has brought a new level of organization and efficiency to our month-end process. We can now track the progress of each task in real-time, allowing us to identify and address bottlenecks quickly. This has not only shortened our close timeline but also reduced the stress and overtime typically associated with period-end activities."

Faster Financial Statement Generation

With the improved data accuracy and streamlined processes, Al Shifa Hospital was able to generate its financial statements much more quickly than before. This early win was particularly appreciated by the hospital's board of directors and external stakeholders who relied on timely financial information.

Dr. Al-Mahmoud highlighted this achievement: "In our first quarter-end close with Oracle Fusion, we were able to present our financial statements to the board five days earlier than our previous average. This improvement in timeliness has been well-received by our stakeholders and has enhanced our reputation for financial transparency and efficiency."

Enhanced Cash Flow Management

Improving cash flow management was a key objective for Al Shifa Hospital in implementing Oracle Fusion, and the early results in this area were particularly encouraging.

Accelerated Accounts Receivable

The Accounts Receivable module of Oracle Fusion provided tools to streamline the billing and collection processes, resulting in faster payment cycles and improved cash flow.

Yousef Al-Nasser, the head of the billing department, reported: "Within the first two months of using Oracle Fusion, we saw a 15% reduction in our average days sales outstanding. The system's automated dunning process and improved visibility into aging receivables have allowed us to follow up on overdue payments more efficiently."

Optimized Accounts Payable

On the payables side, Oracle Fusion's capabilities allowed for better management of vendor payments, taking advantage of early payment discounts while maintaining good relationships with suppliers.

Mariam Al-Hashemi, the procurement manager, noted: "The improved visibility into our payables has allowed us to optimize our payment timing. We've been able to capture more early payment discounts, resulting in cost savings of approximately 2% on our total payables in the first quarter post-implementation."

Improved Cash Forecasting

The Cash Management module of Oracle Fusion provided sophisticated tools for cash forecasting, allowing the finance team to more accurately predict cash inflows and outflows.

Khalid Al-Farsi, the treasury manager, shared his experience: "The cash forecasting capabilities of Oracle Fusion have significantly improved our ability to manage liquidity. In our first month using the system, we were able to reduce our safety cash buffer by 10% without increasing liquidity risk, freeing up capital for other strategic initiatives."

Increased Operational Efficiency

The implementation of Oracle Fusion brought about notable improvements in operational efficiency across various financial processes at Al Shifa Hospital.

Automated Journal Entries

The system's ability to automate recurring journal entries and allocations saved significant time for the accounting team and reduced the risk of manual errors.

Fatima Al-Sayed, a staff accountant, remarked: "The automation of our monthly accruals and depreciation entries has been a huge time-saver. What used to take us several hours each month is now completed automatically with greater accuracy."

Streamlined Approval Processes

Oracle Fusion's workflow capabilities allowed for the implementation of electronic approval processes, replacing the previous paper-based system and significantly reducing processing times.

Ahmed Al-Zaabi, the accounts payable supervisor, noted: "The electronic approval workflow has cut our invoice processing time by half. Approvers can now review and authorize payments from anywhere, even when they're off-site, which has eliminated many of the delays we used to experience."

Improved Intercompany Transactions

For a complex organization like Al Shifa Hospital, with multiple departments and cost centers, the handling of intercompany transactions was greatly simplified by Oracle Fusion.

Laila Khalid commented: "The automated intercompany reconciliation feature has been a game-changer for us. What used to be a major headache at every period-end is now largely automated, saving us countless hours and improving the accuracy of our internal financial reporting."

Enhanced Compliance and Control

Improving financial compliance and control was a key objective for Al Shifa Hospital, and the early results in this area were particularly encouraging.

Stronger Audit Trail

Oracle Fusion's comprehensive audit trail functionality provided a detailed record of all financial transactions and system changes, enhancing transparency and facilitating both internal and external audits.

Nasser Al-Qasimi shared: "In our first internal audit after implementing Oracle Fusion, we were able to provide detailed transaction histories and change logs with ease. This level of transparency has significantly improved our auditors' confidence in our financial controls."

Improved Segregation of Duties

The system's role-based access controls allowed for better segregation of duties, a critical aspect of financial control and compliance.

Amira Saeed noted: "Oracle Fusion has allowed us to implement much more granular access controls. We can now ensure that employees only have access to the specific functions they need, reducing the risk of fraud and improving our overall control environment."

Enhanced Regulatory Reporting

The flexibility of Oracle Fusion's reporting capabilities made it easier for Al Shifa Hospital to meet its various regulatory reporting requirements.

Dr. Al-Mahmoud commented: "The system's ability to generate custom reports has greatly simplified our regulatory reporting process. We can now produce reports tailored to specific regulatory requirements with minimal manual intervention, improving both accuracy and efficiency."

Improved Decision-Making Capabilities

One of the most significant early wins from the Oracle Fusion implementation was the enhanced ability to make data-driven decisions across the organization.

Advanced Analytics

Oracle Fusion's advanced analytics capabilities provided hospital leadership with deeper insights into financial trends and performance metrics.

Ahmed Hassan shared his experience: "The predictive analytics features have been eye-opening. We're now able to forecast patient volumes and associated revenues with much greater accuracy, which has significantly improved our budgeting and resource allocation processes."

Cost Center Profitability Analysis

The system's ability to allocate costs and revenues to specific cost centers provided valuable insights into the profitability of different departments and services.

Dr. Fatima Al-Mahmoud noted: "Within the first quarter of using Oracle Fusion, we identified two service lines that were underperforming financially. This insight allowed us to make timely adjustments to improve their profitability."

Scenario Planning

Oracle Fusion's scenario planning tools allowed the finance team to model different financial scenarios and their potential impacts on the hospital's bottom line.

Khalid Al-Farsi remarked: "The scenario planning capabilities have transformed our strategic planning process. We can now quickly model the financial impact of various strategic initiatives, which has greatly improved the quality of our decision-making at the executive level."

Improved Collaboration and Communication

The implementation of Oracle Fusion fostered improved collaboration and communication among different departments within Al Shifa Hospital.

Cross-Departmental Visibility

The centralized nature of Oracle Fusion allowed for greater transparency across departments, fostering a more collaborative approach to financial management.

Yousef Al-Nasser shared: "The improved visibility has really broken down silos between departments. For example, our billing team now has real-time insights into patient admissions and discharges, allowing us to bill more accurately and quickly."

Standardized Financial Language

The implementation of Oracle Fusion helped establish a common financial language across the organization, improving communication and reducing misunderstandings.

Mariam Al-Hashemi noted: "Having a single source of truth for our financial data has eliminated many of the discrepancies we used to encounter when different departments used different systems or definitions. This has greatly improved our interdepartmental communication and collaboration."

Collaborative Budgeting Process

Oracle Fusion's budgeting tools facilitated a more collaborative approach to the annual budgeting process, involving input from various department heads.

Ahmed Al-Zaabi commented: "Our first budgeting cycle with Oracle Fusion was remarkably smooth. The collaborative features allowed department heads to input their budget requests directly into the system, providing real-time visibility into the overall budget as it was being developed."

Reduced IT Complexity

The move to Oracle Fusion also brought about significant benefits from an IT perspective, reducing the complexity of the hospital's financial systems landscape.

Consolidated Systems

By replacing multiple legacy systems with a single, integrated platform, Al Shifa Hospital was able to significantly reduce its IT footprint.

Hassan Al-Mansouri, the IT Director, shared: "The consolidation of our financial systems into Oracle Fusion has dramatically simplified our IT landscape. We've been able to decommission five legacy systems, reducing our maintenance costs and simplifying our support processes."

Cloud-Based Advantages

As a cloud-based solution, Oracle Fusion eliminated the need for on-premises hardware and reduced the burden on the hospital's IT team for system maintenance and upgrades.

Al-Mansouri added: "The cloud-based nature of Oracle Fusion has been a game-changer for our IT team. We no longer have to worry about hardware upgrades or system patches. This has freed up our team to focus on more strategic initiatives that add value to the hospital."

Improved System Performance

The modern architecture of Oracle Fusion resulted in improved system performance and reliability compared to the hospital's previous financial systems.

Laila Khalid noted: "The speed and responsiveness of Oracle Fusion have been impressive. Tasks that used to take minutes to complete in our old system are now done in seconds. This has not only improved efficiency but also user satisfaction across the finance department."

Enhanced User Experience

The implementation of Oracle Fusion brought about a significant improvement in the user experience for Al Shifa Hospital's finance team and other system users.

Intuitive User Interface

Oracle Fusion's modern, intuitive user interface made it easier for staff to navigate the system and perform their daily tasks efficiently.

Fatima Al-Sayed shared her experience: "The user interface of Oracle Fusion is so much more intuitive than our old system. I was able to learn my way around the basic functions within a day, and the more advanced features were easy to pick up with minimal training."

Mobile Accessibility

The ability to access Oracle Fusion from mobile devices provided greater flexibility for users, particularly for approvals and quick data lookups.

Ahmed Al-Zaabi commented: "The mobile accessibility has been a huge advantage. I can now approve invoices or check financial data on the go, which has greatly improved our responsiveness and decision-making speed."

Personalized Dashboards

The ability for users to customize their dashboards and reports according to their specific needs and preferences was well-received across the organization.

Amira Saeed noted: "The personalized dashboards have been a hit with our team. Everyone can set up their workspace to show the information most relevant to their role, which has improved productivity and job satisfaction."

Conclusion

The early wins realized by Al Shifa Hospital following the implementation of Oracle Fusion were both numerous and significant. From improved financial visibility and streamlined processes to enhanced decision-making capabilities and user experiences, the benefits of the new system were felt across the organization.

These immediate improvements not only validated the decision to implement Oracle Fusion but also set the stage for continued optimization and value realization in the future. The finance team, armed with more accurate and timely information, was now better positioned to support the hospital's strategic objectives and drive financial performance.

As Dr. Fatima Al-Mahmoud reflected on the early successes, she remarked, "The immediate benefits we've seen from Oracle Fusion have exceeded our expectations. While we anticipated improvements in efficiency and accuracy, the breadth and depth of the positive impact across our financial operations have been truly remarkable. These early wins have energized our team and reinforced our commitment to leveraging this powerful tool to its fullest potential."

With these early wins providing a strong foundation, Al Shifa Hospital was well-positioned to continue its journey of financial transformation. The next chapters would focus on how the hospital built upon these initial successes, leveraging Oracle Fusion's advanced capabilities to drive further improvements in financial management, strategic decision-making, and ultimately, patient care.

Chapter 16 - Reporting and Analytics: Gaining Financial Insights

Introduction

As Al Shifa Hospital's implementation of Oracle Fusion Financials reached its maturity, the true power of the system began to emerge through its robust reporting and analytics capabilities. This chapter explores how these features have transformed the hospital's ability to gain valuable financial insights, make data-driven decisions, and ultimately improve its overall financial health.

The Power of Real-Time Data

One of the most significant advantages that Oracle Fusion brought to Al Shifa Hospital was the ability to access real-time financial data. Gone were the days of waiting for month-end reports or struggling with outdated information. The hospital's financial team could now tap into a wealth of up-to-the-minute data, allowing them to make informed decisions quickly and confidently.

Case Study: Emergency Department Resource Allocation

Dr. Fatima, the head of Al Shifa's Emergency Department, had long struggled with optimizing staffing levels during peak hours. With Oracle Fusion's real-time reporting, she could now correlate patient influx data with associated costs, allowing her to adjust staffing levels dynamically. This resulted in a 15% reduction in overtime costs while maintaining high-quality patient care.

Customizable Dashboards: A Window into Financial Health

Oracle Fusion's customizable dashboards proved to be a game-changer for Al Shifa's leadership team. These interactive displays provided at-a-glance views of key financial metrics, allowing executives to monitor the hospital's financial pulse continuously.

Key Dashboard Components

1. Revenue Trends: Daily, weekly, and monthly revenue comparisons
2. Expense Analysis: Breakdown of major expense categories
3. Cash Flow Indicators: Real-time cash position and projections
4. Accounts Receivable Aging: Visual representation of outstanding payments
5. Key Performance Indicators (KPIs): Custom metrics specific to Al Shifa's goals

Drill-Down Capabilities: From Big Picture to Granular Details

While high level overviews were crucial, the true power of Oracle Fusion's reporting lay in its drill-down capabilities. Users could seamlessly navigate from summary data to transaction-level details, providing unprecedented visibility into the hospital's financial operations.

Example: Investigating Cost Variances

When reviewing the monthly expense report, CFO Amir noticed a significant variance in medical supplies costs. Using Oracle Fusion's drill-down feature, he was able to:

1. Identify the specific departments contributing to the variance
2. Pinpoint the exact products causing the cost increase
3. Review individual purchase orders and supplier agreements

This level of detail allowed Amir to address the issue promptly, negotiating better rates with suppliers and implementing stricter purchasing controls where necessary.

Advanced Analytics: Unleashing the Power of Predictive Insights

Beyond traditional reporting, Oracle Fusion's advanced analytics capabilities opened up new possibilities for Al Shifa Hospital. By leveraging historical data and sophisticated algorithms, the system could generate predictive insights, helping the hospital anticipate future financial trends and challenges.

Predictive Analytics in Action

1. Revenue Forecasting: By analyzing historical patient data, seasonal trends, and external factors, Oracle Fusion could generate accurate revenue forecasts, allowing for more precise budgeting and resource allocation.
2. Cash Flow Projection: The system's ability to predict cash flow based on historical patterns and upcoming financial obligations helped Al Shifa maintain optimal liquidity levels.
3. Bad Debt Prediction: By identifying patterns in patient payment behaviors, the hospital could proactively address potential bad debt situations, improving overall collection rates.

Benchmarking and Comparative Analysis

Oracle Fusion's reporting tools also allowed Al Shifa Hospital to benchmark its financial performance against industry standards and peer institutions. This comparative analysis provided valuable context for the hospital's financial metrics and highlighted areas for improvement.

Benchmarking Metrics

1. Operating Margin
2. Days in Accounts Receivable
3. Salary and Benefit Expense as a Percentage of Net Patient Revenue
4. Supply Expense per Adjusted Patient Day
5. Average Length of Stay

By comparing these metrics to industry benchmarks, Al Shifa's leadership could identify areas where they excelled and where they needed to focus improvement efforts.

Financial Planning and Analysis: Scenario Modeling

Oracle Fusion's robust reporting and analytics capabilities extended beyond historical and current data analysis. The system's scenario modeling features allowed Al Shifa's financial team to project the impact of various decisions and external factors on the hospital's financial future.

Case Study: Expansion Project Financial Analysis

When considering the addition of a new wing to the hospital, the finance team used Oracle Fusion to model various scenarios:

1. Base Case: Projected financials without the expansion
2. Conservative Expansion: Assuming lower-than-expected patient volume
3. Aggressive Expansion: Modeling higher patient volume and additional services
4. Phased Expansion: Analyzing the impact of a gradual rollout

These models provided crucial insights that informed the hospital's decision-making process, ultimately leading to a more confident and data-driven expansion strategy.

Streamlined Compliance Reporting

In the heavily regulated healthcare industry, compliance reporting is a critical aspect of financial management. Oracle Fusion's reporting capabilities significantly streamlined this process for Al Shifa Hospital, ensuring accuracy and timeliness in regulatory submissions.

Automated Compliance Reports

1. Financial Statements: Balance sheets, income statements, and cash flow statements generated automatically, ensuring consistency and reducing manual errors.
2. Tax Reports: Simplified tax reporting with built-in compliance checks and automatic calculations.
3. Regulatory Filings: Streamlined generation of reports required by health authorities and government agencies.
4. Audit Trail Reports: Detailed logs of all financial transactions and system access, facilitating internal and external audits.

Mobile Access: Insights on the Go

Recognizing the need for flexibility in accessing financial information, Oracle Fusion's mobile capabilities allowed Al Shifa's leadership to view critical reports and dashboards on their smartphones and tablets. This feature proved invaluable for making quick decisions, even when executives were away from their desks.

Mobile Reporting Features

1. Real-time KPI updates
2. Ability to drill down into data
3. Approval workflows for time-sensitive financial decisions
4. Secure access to financial information

Collaborative Reporting: Breaking Down Silos

Oracle Fusion's collaborative reporting features fostered greater communication and cooperation between different departments at Al Shifa Hospital. The ability to share reports, add comments, and collaborate on financial analysis broke down traditional silos, leading to more holistic decision-making.

Interdepartmental Collaboration Example

When analyzing the profitability of different medical services, the finance team could easily share their findings with department heads. This collaborative approach allowed for a more nuanced understanding of the financial data, incorporating clinical perspectives that might not be immediately apparent from the numbers alone.

Data Visualization: Making Numbers Come to Life

While robust data and advanced analytics were crucial, Oracle Fusion's data visualization capabilities truly brought the financial insights to life. Complex financial concepts could now be communicated clearly and effectively through intuitive charts, graphs, and interactive visualizations.

Visualization Examples

1. Heat maps showing profitability by department or service line
2. Waterfall charts illustrating the components of revenue growth
3. Bubble charts comparing volume, revenue, and profitability of different procedures
4. Interactive Sankey diagrams depicting cash flow through the organization

These visualizations not only made financial data more accessible to non-financial stakeholders but also revealed patterns and trends that might have been missed in traditional tabular reports.

Continuous Improvement through Analytics

As Al Shifa Hospital became more proficient in leveraging Oracle Fusion's reporting and analytics capabilities, a culture of continuous improvement began to take root. Regular review of key metrics and ongoing analysis of financial data became integral to the hospital's operations.

Continuous Improvement Initiatives

1. Weekly financial performance reviews with department heads
2. Monthly deep-dive analytics sessions to identify cost-saving opportunities
3. Quarterly benchmarking exercises to track progress against industry standards
4. Annual strategic planning informed by comprehensive financial analysis

Challenges and Lessons Learned

While Oracle Fusion's reporting and analytics capabilities brought significant benefits to Al Shifa Hospital, the journey was not without its challenges. Some key lessons learned include:

1. Data Quality is Paramount: The accuracy of reports and analytics is only as good as the data input into the system. Establishing strict data entry protocols and regular audits was crucial.
2. User Training is Ongoing: As new features and reports were developed, ongoing training was necessary to ensure all users could effectively leverage the system's capabilities.
3. Balancing Standardization and Customization: While Oracle Fusion offered a wealth of standard reports, finding the right balance between using out-of-the-box solutions and developing custom reports was an ongoing process.
4. Managing Information Overload: With so much data available, it was important to focus on the most relevant metrics and avoid overwhelming users with unnecessary information.

Future Directions: Artificial Intelligence and Machine Learning

As Al Shifa Hospital looked to the future, the potential integration of artificial intelligence (AI) and machine learning (ML) into Oracle Fusion's reporting and analytics capabilities held exciting possibilities. These technologies could further enhance the system's predictive capabilities and automate complex financial analyses.

Potential AI/ML Applications

1. Anomaly Detection: Automatically identifying unusual

financial patterns or transactions that may require attention.

2. Natural Language Processing: Allowing users to query financial data using natural language, making insights more accessible to non-technical users.
3. Predictive Maintenance: Using financial and operational data to predict when medical equipment might need maintenance or replacement, optimizing capital expenditure.
4. Patient Payment Behavior Analysis: Leveraging ML algorithms to predict patient payment patterns and optimize collection strategies.

Conclusion

Oracle Fusion's reporting and analytics capabilities have fundamentally transformed how Al Shifa Hospital understands and manages its financial health. From real-time dashboards to advanced predictive analytics, these tools have empowered the hospital's leadership to make data-driven decisions, optimize operations, and ultimately provide better patient care.

As Al Shifa continues to explore and leverage these powerful features, the hospital is well-positioned to navigate the complex financial landscape of modern healthcare. The insights gained through Oracle Fusion have not only improved the hospital's bottom line but have also contributed to its mission of delivering high-quality, cost-effective healthcare to the community it serves.

Looking ahead, the potential for even more advanced analytics, powered by AI and ML, promises to further revolutionize financial management in healthcare. Al Shifa Hospital, with its strong foundation in Oracle Fusion's reporting and analytics capabilities, is ready to embrace these future innovations and continue its journey towards financial excellence.

Chapter 17 - Compliance and Auditing: Ensuring Regulatory Adherence

Introduction

As Al Shifa Hospital embarked on its journey to transform its financial operations with Oracle Fusion, one of the most critical aspects to address was compliance and auditing. In the healthcare industry, adherence to regulatory requirements is not just a matter of good practice; it's a fundamental necessity. This chapter explores how Oracle Fusion has helped Al Shifa Hospital meet its regulatory obligations and streamline its auditing processes, ensuring that the hospital maintains its reputation for excellence while navigating the complex landscape of healthcare finance regulations.

The Regulatory Landscape in Healthcare Finance

Overview of Healthcare Financial Regulations

The healthcare industry is subject to a myriad of regulations designed to ensure patient safety, data privacy, and financial transparency. For Al Shifa Hospital, operating in Dubai, this meant navigating both local and international standards. Some of the key regulatory frameworks that the hospital needed to comply with included:

1. Dubai Health Authority (DHA) regulations
2. UAE Federal Law on Medical Liability
3. Health Insurance Portability and Accountability Act (HIPAA) for international patients
4. International Financial Reporting Standards (IFRS)
5. Anti-Money Laundering (AML) and Know Your Customer (KYC) regulations

Each of these regulatory frameworks came with its own set of requirements, reporting standards, and auditing processes. Before the implementation of Oracle Fusion, Al Shifa Hospital struggled to manage these diverse compliance needs efficiently, often relying on manual processes and disparate systems that were prone to errors and inconsistencies.

Challenges Faced by Al Shifa Hospital

Prior to the Oracle Fusion implementation, Al Shifa Hospital faced several compliance and auditing challenges:

1. Time-consuming manual data collection for regulatory reporting
2. Inconsistencies in financial data across different departments
3. Difficulty in tracking and documenting compliance activities
4. Lengthy and complex audit processes
5. Risk of non-compliance due to human error or oversight
6. Lack of real-time visibility into compliance status

These challenges not only posed a risk to the hospital's regulatory standing but also consumed significant time and resources that could have been better utilized in patient care and hospital operations.

Oracle Fusion's Compliance and Auditing Capabilities

Built-in Compliance Features

Oracle Fusion came equipped with a robust set of compliance features designed to address the specific needs of healthcare organizations like Al Shifa Hospital. Some of the key compliance capabilities included:

1. **Automated Compliance Reporting**: Oracle Fusion's

reporting tools allowed for the creation of customized reports that aligned with various regulatory requirements. This automation significantly reduced the time and effort required to prepare compliance reports.

2. **Segregation of Duties**: The system enforced strict access controls and segregation of duties, ensuring that no single individual had excessive control over financial processes. This feature was crucial for preventing fraud and maintaining financial integrity.
3. **Audit Trails**: Every transaction and system change was automatically logged, creating a comprehensive audit trail. This feature proved invaluable during audits and investigations, providing a clear record of all financial activities.
4. **Configurable Workflow Approvals**: Oracle Fusion allowed Al Shifa Hospital to set up approval workflows that aligned with their internal control policies and regulatory requirements. This ensured that all financial transactions went through the appropriate channels before being finalized.
5. **Regulatory Updates**: Oracle regularly provided updates to the system to reflect changes in regulatory requirements, ensuring that Al Shifa Hospital always had access to the most up-to-date compliance tools.

Enhanced Auditing Processes

The implementation of Oracle Fusion also brought about significant improvements in Al Shifa Hospital's auditing processes:

1. **Centralized Data Repository**: All financial data was now stored in a single, centralized system, making it easier for auditors to access and analyze information.

2. **Real-time Monitoring**: The system provided real-time visibility into financial transactions, allowing for continuous monitoring and early detection of potential compliance issues.
3. **Standardized Processes**: Oracle Fusion enforced standardized financial processes across the hospital, reducing the risk of errors and inconsistencies that could complicate audits.
4. **Automated Internal Controls**: The system included automated controls that flagged unusual transactions or potential compliance violations, allowing for prompt investigation and resolution.
5. **Integrated Audit Tools**: Oracle Fusion came with built-in audit tools that streamlined the audit process, allowing auditors to quickly access and analyze the data they needed.

Implementing Compliance and Auditing Features at Al Shifa Hospital

Customizing Oracle Fusion for Al Shifa's Regulatory Needs

While Oracle Fusion came with powerful out-of-the-box compliance features, the implementation team recognized the need to tailor the system to Al Shifa Hospital's specific regulatory environment. This customization process involved several key steps:

1. **Regulatory Gap Analysis**: The team conducted a comprehensive analysis of Al Shifa's regulatory obligations and compared them with Oracle Fusion's capabilities. This helped identify areas where additional customization was needed.
2. **Custom Report Development**: Working closely with the hospital's compliance team, the Oracle consultants developed

custom reports that aligned precisely with the reporting requirements of various regulatory bodies.

3. **Workflow Configuration**: The approval workflows within Oracle Fusion were configured to match Al Shifa's internal control policies and regulatory requirements. This ensured that all financial transactions went through the appropriate approval channels.
4. **User Role Definition**: The team defined user roles and access privileges that reflected the hospital's organizational structure and segregation of duties requirements.
5. **Integration with Local Systems**: Oracle Fusion was integrated with local systems specific to UAE healthcare regulations, ensuring seamless compliance with regional requirements.

Training and Change Management

Implementing new compliance and auditing processes required significant changes in how Al Shifa Hospital's staff approached their work. To ensure a smooth transition, the implementation team developed a comprehensive training and change management program:

1. **Role-based Training**: Different training modules were developed for various user groups, focusing on the compliance aspects most relevant to their roles.
2. **Compliance Awareness Sessions**: Regular sessions were held to educate staff about the importance of compliance and how Oracle Fusion supported regulatory adherence.
3. **Hands-on Workshops**: Practical workshops allowed staff to familiarize themselves with the new compliance and auditing features in a safe, test environment.

4. **Ongoing Support**: A dedicated support team was established to assist users with compliance-related queries and issues during and after the implementation.
5. **Regular Updates**: As regulatory requirements evolved, the training program was updated to ensure staff remained informed about new compliance features and processes.

Real-world Impact: Compliance and Auditing at Al Shifa Hospital Post-Implementation

Streamlined Regulatory Reporting

One of the most immediate benefits Al Shifa Hospital experienced was a significant reduction in the time and effort required for regulatory reporting. Dr. Aisha Mahmoud, the hospital's Compliance Officer, shared her experience:

"Before Oracle Fusion, preparing our quarterly compliance reports for the Dubai Health Authority was a nightmare. We'd spend weeks collecting data from different departments, reconciling discrepancies, and manually compiling reports. Now, with Oracle Fusion, we can generate these reports at the click of a button. What used to take weeks now takes hours, and the accuracy of our reports has improved dramatically."

The automated reporting capabilities of Oracle Fusion not only saved time but also reduced the risk of errors in regulatory submissions. This improvement in reporting efficiency and accuracy helped Al Shifa Hospital build stronger relationships with regulatory bodies and enhance its reputation for compliance.

Enhanced Audit Readiness

The implementation of Oracle Fusion significantly improved Al Shifa Hospital's audit readiness. Mr. Tariq Al-Hashemi, the hospital's Chief Financial Officer, noted the difference during their annual external audit:

"Our first external audit after implementing Oracle Fusion was a completely different experience. In the past, audits were stressful events that disrupted our operations for weeks. With Oracle Fusion, we were able to provide auditors with direct access to the system, allowing them to retrieve the information they needed quickly and easily. The audit was completed in half the time compared to previous years, and the auditors commented on the transparency and completeness of our financial records."

The centralized data repository and comprehensive audit trails provided by Oracle Fusion not only expedited the audit process but also improved the quality of audits. Auditors were able to conduct more thorough reviews, giving stakeholders greater confidence in the hospital's financial management.

Improved Internal Controls

Oracle Fusion's automated internal controls had a significant impact on Al Shifa Hospital's ability to prevent and detect compliance issues. Ms. Fatima Al-Suwaidi, the Internal Audit Manager, shared an example:

"About three months after go-live, the system flagged an unusual pattern of transactions in our accounts payable department. Thanks to the real-time monitoring capabilities of Oracle Fusion, we were able to investigate immediately. It turned out to be a simple processing error, but in the past, this might have gone unnoticed for months. The early detection allowed us to correct the issue quickly and prevent any compliance violations."

This proactive approach to compliance, enabled by Oracle Fusion's automated controls and monitoring features, helped Al Shifa Hospital maintain a strong compliance posture and reduce the risk of regulatory violations.

Simplified Compliance with International Standards

As Al Shifa Hospital continued to expand its services to international patients, compliance with global standards like HIPAA became increasingly important. Dr. Omar Al-Mansouri, the hospital's Chief Information Officer, explained how Oracle Fusion supported this:

"Oracle Fusion's robust security features and data protection capabilities have been crucial in helping us comply with international standards like HIPAA. The system's ability to encrypt sensitive data, control access based on user roles, and maintain detailed audit logs has given us confidence in our ability to protect patient information in line with global best practices."

This enhanced capability to comply with international standards not only reduced regulatory risks but also opened up new opportunities for Al Shifa Hospital to attract international patients and partnerships.

Overcoming Challenges in Compliance and Auditing Implementation

While the overall implementation of Oracle Fusion's compliance and auditing features was successful, Al Shifa Hospital did face some challenges along the way. Understanding these challenges and how they were overcome provides valuable insights for other healthcare organizations considering similar implementations.

Challenge 1: Resistance to Change

One of the initial challenges was resistance from staff who were accustomed to the old ways of managing compliance and auditing tasks. Many were apprehensive about learning a new system and feared that the automation might make their roles redundant.

Solution: The implementation team addressed this challenge through a combination of clear communication and comprehensive training. They organized town hall meetings to explain the benefits of the new system, not just for the hospital but for individual roles as well. They emphasized how automation would free up time for more value-added tasks. The role-based training programs helped staff see how Oracle Fusion would make their jobs easier and more efficient.

Challenge 2: Data Migration and Integrity

Ensuring the accuracy and completeness of historical compliance data during the migration to Oracle Fusion was crucial for maintaining regulatory adherence and audit trails.

Solution: The team adopted a phased approach to data migration. They started with a thorough data cleansing process, identifying and correcting inconsistencies in the existing data. They then used Oracle's data migration tools to transfer the data, followed by extensive validation checks. For critical compliance data, they maintained parallel records for a transition period to ensure nothing was lost in the migration.

Challenge 3: Customization vs. Standardization

Balancing the need for customization to meet Al Shifa Hospital's specific regulatory requirements with the benefits of using standardized processes was a significant challenge.

Solution: The implementation team worked closely with Oracle consultants to find the right balance. They identified core compliance processes that could be managed using standard Oracle Fusion features and focused customization efforts on areas with unique local regulatory requirements. This approach allowed Al Shifa to benefit from Oracle's ongoing updates to standard features while maintaining the flexibility to meet specific local needs.

Challenge 4: Keeping Pace with Regulatory Changes

Healthcare regulations are constantly evolving, and there was concern about how to keep the system updated with these changes.

Solution: The hospital established a dedicated compliance team responsible for monitoring regulatory changes. This team worked closely with Oracle to ensure that the system was regularly updated to reflect new requirements. They also developed a process for quickly implementing and testing new compliance features or reports as needed.

The Future of Compliance and Auditing at Al Shifa Hospital

As Al Shifa Hospital continues to leverage Oracle Fusion for its compliance and auditing needs, several exciting possibilities for the future have emerged:

Artificial Intelligence and Machine Learning

The hospital is exploring the potential of AI and machine learning capabilities within Oracle Fusion to enhance its compliance efforts. These technologies could be used to:

1. Predict potential compliance issues before they occur

2. Automatically detect anomalies in financial transactions that might indicate fraud or errors
3. Continuously optimize internal controls based on historical data and patterns

Blockchain for Auditing

Al Shifa Hospital is considering the integration of blockchain technology with Oracle Fusion to further enhance the integrity and traceability of its financial records. This could provide an immutable audit trail that would significantly simplify the auditing process and increase stakeholder trust.

Continuous Auditing

With the real-time data access provided by Oracle Fusion, Al Shifa Hospital is moving towards a model of continuous auditing. Rather than conducting large, periodic audits, the hospital aims to implement ongoing monitoring and smaller, more frequent audits. This approach could help identify and address issues more quickly and reduce the disruption caused by large-scale audits.

Enhanced Reporting Capabilities

As regulatory requirements continue to evolve, Al Shifa Hospital plans to leverage Oracle Fusion's advanced analytics and reporting capabilities to develop more sophisticated compliance reports. These could include predictive compliance indicators and real-time compliance dashboards for hospital leadership.

Conclusion

The implementation of Oracle Fusion has transformed compliance and auditing processes at Al Shifa Hospital, turning what was once a cumbersome and time-consuming aspect of financial management into a streamlined, efficient, and value-adding function. By providing robust compliance features, enhancing audit readiness, and improving internal controls, Oracle Fusion has helped Al Shifa Hospital not only meet its regulatory obligations but also gain a competitive advantage in the healthcare market.

As regulations continue to evolve and the healthcare landscape becomes increasingly complex, the flexibility and scalability of Oracle Fusion position Al Shifa Hospital well for the future. The hospital's journey demonstrates that with the right technology and approach, compliance and auditing can move beyond being mere regulatory requirements to become powerful tools for driving operational excellence and building stakeholder trust.

As we look ahead to the continuous improvement efforts at Al Shifa Hospital, it's clear that the strong foundation laid by Oracle Fusion in compliance and auditing will play a crucial role in the hospital's ongoing financial success and its ability to deliver high-quality patient care.

Chapter 18 - Continuous Improvement: Leveraging Oracle Fusion's Full Potential

Introduction

As Al Shifa Hospital settles into its new Oracle Fusion system, the journey towards financial excellence is far from over. In fact, it's just beginning. This chapter explores the ongoing efforts to optimize the use of Oracle Fusion and drive further financial improvements at the hospital. We'll delve into the strategies, processes, and mindset shifts required to ensure that Al Shifa Hospital continues to leverage Oracle Fusion's full potential, long after the initial implementation.

The Continuous Improvement Mindset

Embracing a Culture of Ongoing Enhancement

The successful implementation of Oracle Fusion at Al Shifa Hospital marked a significant milestone, but it was not the end goal. The hospital's leadership recognized that to truly reap the benefits of this powerful system, they needed to instill a culture of continuous improvement throughout the organization.

Dr. Fatima, the hospital's CEO, spearheaded this initiative by emphasizing the importance of ongoing learning and adaptation. She often reminded her team, "Our journey with Oracle Fusion is like tending to a garden. We've planted the seeds, but now we must nurture and cultivate them to see them flourish."

This mindset shift was crucial in ensuring that the hospital didn't fall into the trap of complacency after the initial excitement of the implementation wore off. Instead, it set the stage for a long-term commitment to leveraging Oracle Fusion's capabilities to their fullest extent.

Establishing a Dedicated Improvement Team

To drive this continuous improvement effort, Al Shifa Hospital established a dedicated team responsible for identifying and implementing ongoing enhancements to the Oracle Fusion system. This cross-functional team, dubbed the "Fusion Excellence Team," included representatives from finance, IT, and various clinical departments.

The team's primary objectives were to:

1. Monitor system performance and user feedback
2. Identify areas for improvement and optimization
3. Research and propose new features or modules that could benefit the hospital
4. Coordinate with Oracle for updates and support
5. Facilitate ongoing training and knowledge sharing

By having a dedicated team focused on these objectives, Al Shifa Hospital ensured that the momentum gained from the initial implementation would not be lost and that the system would continue to evolve alongside the hospital's needs.

Optimizing Existing Modules

Fine-tuning the General Ledger

The General Ledger module, being the backbone of Al Shifa Hospital's financial operations, was a primary focus for optimization efforts. The Fusion Excellence Team worked closely with the finance department to refine the chart of accounts, ensuring it accurately reflected the hospital's evolving organizational structure and reporting needs.

One significant improvement was the implementation of a more granular cost center structure. This allowed for more detailed financial analysis and better allocation of resources across different departments and services. Dr. Ahmed, the CFO, noted, "The enhanced cost center structure has given us unprecedented visibility into our financial performance at a departmental level. This granularity allows us to make more informed decisions about resource allocation and identify areas for cost optimization."

The team also focused on streamlining the month-end close process. By leveraging Oracle Fusion's automation capabilities and refining internal workflows, they managed to reduce the close cycle from seven days to just three, freeing up valuable time for financial analysis and strategic planning.

Enhancing Accounts Receivable Processes

In the Accounts Receivable module, the focus was on improving cash flow and reducing days in accounts receivable (DAR). The team implemented several strategies to achieve these goals:

1. Automated payment reminders: Leveraging Oracle Fusion's communication tools, the hospital set up an automated system to send timely reminders to patients and insurance companies about outstanding balances.
2. Enhanced reporting: Custom reports were developed to provide real-time insights into receivables aging, allowing the finance team to proactively address potential collection issues.
3. Integration with patient portals: By integrating Oracle Fusion with the hospital's patient portal, patients could now view their bills and make payments online, significantly improving the collection process.
4. Machine learning for predicting payment behavior: The team worked with Oracle to implement machine learning algorithms that could predict payment behavior based on

historical data, allowing for more targeted collection efforts.

These enhancements resulted in a 20% reduction in DAR within six months of implementation, significantly improving the hospital's cash position.

Optimizing Accounts Payable

On the Accounts Payable side, the focus was on improving vendor relationships and maximizing early payment discounts. The Fusion Excellence Team implemented several improvements:

1. Automated invoice matching: By fine-tuning the system's invoice matching capabilities, the hospital significantly reduced the time spent on manual invoice processing and increased the percentage of invoices processed without human intervention.
2. Dynamic discounting: The team implemented Oracle Fusion's dynamic discounting feature, which allowed the hospital to take advantage of early payment discounts based on its current cash position.
3. Vendor portal enhancements: The vendor portal was optimized to provide suppliers with real-time visibility into invoice and payment status, reducing the number of inquiries and improving vendor satisfaction.
4. Payment optimization: By analyzing payment patterns and vendor terms, the team developed a strategy to optimize payment timing, balancing cash flow management with vendor relationships and discount opportunities.

These improvements resulted in a 15% reduction in processing costs and a 30% increase in early payment discount capture.

Maximizing Fixed Assets Management

In the Fixed Assets module, the focus was on improving asset tracking and maintenance scheduling. The team implemented several enhancements:

1. RFID integration: By integrating RFID technology with Oracle Fusion, the hospital improved its ability to track and locate valuable medical equipment in real-time.
2. Predictive maintenance: Leveraging Oracle Fusion's analytics capabilities, the team developed predictive maintenance models that helped optimize equipment uptime and reduce unexpected breakdowns.
3. Asset utilization analysis: Custom reports were created to analyze asset utilization rates, helping the hospital make informed decisions about equipment purchases and allocations.
4. Enhanced depreciation forecasting: The team fine-tuned the system's depreciation calculations and forecasting capabilities, providing more accurate long-term financial projections.

These improvements led to a 25% reduction in equipment downtime and a 10% decrease in unnecessary equipment purchases.

Exploring New Modules and Features

Implementing Oracle Fusion Expenses

As Al Shifa Hospital continued to grow, managing employee expenses became increasingly complex. The Fusion Excellence Team recognized an opportunity to streamline this process by implementing Oracle Fusion Expenses.

The implementation process involved:

1. Configuring expense categories and policies to align with hospital regulations
2. Integrating with the hospital's HR system for employee data
3. Setting up approval workflows tailored to the hospital's organizational structure
4. Training employees on the new mobile app for expense submission

Dr. Fatima commented on the impact of this new module: "Oracle Fusion Expenses has transformed our expense management process. It's not just about saving time and reducing errors; it's about giving our staff the tools they need to focus on what really matters – patient care."

The implementation of Oracle Fusion Expenses resulted in a 40% reduction in expense processing time and a 60% decrease in policy violations.

Exploring Oracle Fusion Risk Management

As the hospital's operations grew more complex, managing risk became increasingly important. The Fusion Excellence Team began exploring the potential of Oracle Fusion Risk Management to enhance the hospital's risk management capabilities.

Key areas of focus included:

1. Financial risk management: Implementing tools to monitor and mitigate financial risks, including currency fluctuations and credit risks.
2. Compliance management: Leveraging the module's capabilities to ensure adherence to healthcare regulations and standards.
3. Operational risk management: Identifying and mitigating risks in day-to-day hospital operations, from patient safety to

supply chain disruptions.
4. Audit management: Streamlining the audit process and ensuring continuous compliance with internal and external requirements.

While still in the early stages of exploration, the potential benefits of implementing this module were clear. Dr. Ahmed noted, "In today's complex healthcare environment, robust risk management is not just a nice-to-have; it's a necessity. Oracle Fusion Risk Management could provide us with the comprehensive view we need to navigate these challenges effectively."

Leveraging Advanced Analytics and Reporting

Implementing Predictive Analytics

As Al Shifa Hospital became more comfortable with Oracle Fusion's basic reporting capabilities, the Fusion Excellence Team began to explore more advanced analytics features. They focused on implementing predictive analytics to drive proactive decision-making across various aspects of hospital operations.

Some key areas where predictive analytics were applied included:

1. Patient admission forecasting: By analyzing historical data and external factors like local events and weather patterns, the hospital could more accurately predict patient admissions, allowing for better staff and resource allocation.
2. Revenue cycle optimization: Predictive models were developed to identify potential delays or issues in the revenue cycle, allowing the finance team to take proactive measures to ensure timely payments.
3. Supply chain management: Analytics were used to optimize inventory levels and predict potential supply chain

disruptions, ensuring the hospital always had the necessary supplies on hand without overstocking.

4. Staff scheduling: By analyzing patient flow patterns and staff performance data, the hospital could optimize staff schedules to ensure appropriate coverage while minimizing overtime costs.

Dr. Fatima expressed her excitement about these developments: "Predictive analytics is like having a crystal ball for our hospital. It allows us to anticipate challenges and opportunities, rather than just reacting to them. This proactive approach is transforming how we operate and deliver care."

Developing Custom Dashboards

To make the wealth of data generated by Oracle Fusion more accessible and actionable, the Fusion Excellence Team worked on developing custom dashboards tailored to different roles within the hospital.

These dashboards included:

1. Executive Dashboard: Providing high-level KPIs and trends for hospital leadership, including financial performance, patient satisfaction scores, and operational efficiency metrics.
2. Department-specific Dashboards: Tailored views for each department, highlighting relevant metrics and performance indicators.
3. Clinician Dashboard: Offering insights into patient care metrics, resource utilization, and financial performance related to individual clinicians or specialties.
4. Finance Dashboard: Detailed financial metrics, including real-time cash flow updates, accounts receivable aging, and budget variance analysis.

The implementation of these custom dashboards significantly improved data visibility and decision-making across the organization. Dr. Ahmed noted, "These dashboards have democratized data within our organization. Everyone now has access to the insights they need to make informed decisions in their respective roles."

Continuous Learning and Skill Development

Ongoing Training Programs

Recognizing that the success of Oracle Fusion depended on the skills of its users, Al Shifa Hospital implemented a comprehensive ongoing training program. This program went beyond the initial implementation training, focusing on continuous skill development and knowledge sharing.

Key components of the training program included:

1. Regular refresher courses: Quarterly sessions to reinforce key concepts and introduce new features or updates.
2. Advanced user training: In-depth courses for power users, focusing on advanced features and customization options.
3. Role-specific training: Tailored sessions for different roles within the hospital, ensuring each user understood how to leverage Oracle Fusion effectively in their specific context.
4. Certification program: An internal certification program to recognize and incentivize expertise in Oracle Fusion.
5. Lunch and learn sessions: Informal knowledge-sharing sessions where users could share tips, tricks, and best practices.

Dr. Fatima emphasized the importance of this ongoing training: "Our investment in Oracle Fusion isn't just about the technology; it's about our people. By continually developing their skills, we ensure that we're always getting the most out of the system."

Leveraging Oracle Learning Resources

In addition to internal training programs, Al Shifa Hospital actively encouraged staff to take advantage of Oracle's learning resources. This included:

1. Oracle University courses: Online and in-person courses offered by Oracle to deepen understanding of various Oracle Fusion modules.
2. Oracle Cloud Customer Connect: An online community where users could share experiences, ask questions, and learn from other Oracle Fusion users globally.
3. Oracle documentation and knowledge base: Encouraging staff to explore Oracle's extensive documentation and troubleshooting resources.
4. Oracle conferences and webinars: Sponsoring staff attendance at Oracle events to learn about upcoming features and industry best practices.

By leveraging these resources, Al Shifa Hospital ensured that its staff stayed up-to-date with the latest developments in Oracle Fusion and could continue to push the boundaries of what was possible with the system.

Fostering Innovation

Encouraging User-driven Innovation

The Fusion Excellence Team recognized that some of the best ideas for improvement could come from the day-to-day users of the system. To tap into this potential, they implemented several initiatives to encourage user-driven innovation:

1. Innovation challenges: Quarterly challenges where staff could submit ideas for new ways to use Oracle Fusion or suggestions for improvements.
2. Fusion Feedback Forum: A regular meeting where users could share their experiences, challenges, and ideas directly with the Fusion Excellence Team.
3. Idea Management System: An online platform integrated with Oracle Fusion where users could submit, vote on, and discuss improvement ideas.
4. Recognition program: A program to recognize and reward staff members who contributed innovative ideas or solutions.

These initiatives not only generated valuable ideas for improvement but also increased user engagement and ownership of the Oracle Fusion system. As one nurse put it, "It's great to know that our ideas are valued. It makes us feel like we're part of the ongoing evolution of the system."

Collaboration with Oracle

Al Shifa Hospital also fostered a close collaborative relationship with Oracle, participating in various programs to drive innovation:

1. Beta testing: Volunteering to beta test new features and modules, providing valuable feedback to Oracle and gaining early access to new capabilities.
2. Customer advisory board: Participating in Oracle's customer advisory board, influencing the future direction of Oracle Fusion development.
3. Co-innovation projects: Collaborating with Oracle on specific projects to develop new features or capabilities tailored to the healthcare industry.

4. Case studies and speaking engagements: Sharing Al Shifa Hospital's success stories and learnings with the broader Oracle community through case studies and conference presentations.

This close collaboration not only benefited Al Shifa Hospital but also contributed to the broader evolution of Oracle Fusion for healthcare organizations globally.

Measuring and Communicating Success

Developing a Comprehensive KPI Framework

To ensure that the continuous improvement efforts were delivering tangible results, the Fusion Excellence Team developed a comprehensive Key Performance Indicator (KPI) framework. This framework included metrics across various dimensions:

1. Financial metrics: Including days in accounts receivable, cost per patient day, revenue cycle efficiency, and budget variance.
2. Operational metrics: Such as system uptime, transaction processing times, and user adoption rates.
3. User satisfaction metrics: Measured through regular surveys and feedback sessions.
4. Innovation metrics: Tracking the number of improvement ideas submitted, implemented, and their impact.
5. Training and skill development metrics: Including training completion rates, certification levels, and knowledge assessment scores.

This KPI framework provided a holistic view of the impact of Oracle Fusion on Al Shifa Hospital's operations and guided future improvement efforts.

Regular Communication and Celebration of Wins

The Fusion Excellence Team recognized the importance of regularly communicating progress and celebrating successes to maintain momentum and engagement. They implemented several communication channels:

1. Monthly newsletter: Highlighting recent improvements, upcoming features, and success stories.
2. Quarterly town halls: Presenting key metrics, major achievements, and future plans to all staff.
3. Success story database: A searchable repository of case studies showcasing how different departments leveraged Oracle Fusion to improve their operations.
4. Recognition events: Regular events to recognize and celebrate individuals and teams who made significant contributions to the continuous improvement effort.

Dr. Fatima emphasized the importance of this communication: "By regularly sharing our progress and celebrating our wins, we keep everyone engaged and excited about the possibilities of Oracle Fusion. It's not just a system; it's a journey we're all on together."

Conclusion

As Al Shifa Hospital continues its journey with Oracle Fusion, the focus on continuous improvement ensures that the system remains a dynamic, evolving tool that drives ongoing financial and operational excellence. By fostering a culture of innovation, investing in ongoing learning, and maintaining a close partnership with Oracle, the hospital is well-positioned to leverage Oracle Fusion's full potential for years to come.

Dr. Ahmed reflected on the journey so far: "Implementing Oracle Fusion was just the beginning. It's our commitment to continuous improvement that's truly transforming our hospital. We're not just using a system; we're constantly pushing the boundaries of what's possible in healthcare finance and operations."

As Al Shifa Hospital looks to the future, the possibilities seem endless. With a solid foundation in Oracle Fusion and a dedicated team driving continuous improvement, the hospital is well-equipped to navigate the evolving healthcare landscape and continue delivering exceptional patient care.

Chapter 19 - ROI Analysis: Measuring the Impact

Introduction

As Al Shifa Hospital's journey with Oracle Fusion Financials reaches a critical milestone, it's time to evaluate the return on investment (ROI) and measure the overall impact of this transformative implementation. This chapter delves into a comprehensive analysis of the financial and operational benefits realized by the hospital since the adoption of Oracle Fusion. We'll explore various metrics, compare pre- and post-implementation data, and quantify the value added to Al Shifa's operations.

Establishing the Baseline

Before we can accurately measure the impact of Oracle Fusion, it's crucial to establish a clear baseline of Al Shifa Hospital's financial and operational performance prior to implementation. This provides a reference point against which we can compare the post-implementation results.

Pre-implementation Financial Metrics

To set the stage for our ROI analysis, let's review some key financial metrics from Al Shifa Hospital before the Oracle Fusion implementation:

1. Revenue Cycle Management:

○ Average Days in Accounts Receivable (AR): 65 days

○ Claims Denial Rate: 12%

○ Clean Claims Rate: 75%

2. Cost Management:

○ Operating Margin: 3.5%

○ Supply Chain Costs as % of Operating Expense: 35%

○ Average Days in Accounts Payable (AP): 45 days

3. Financial Reporting:

○ Time to Close Monthly Books: 15 days

○ Accuracy of Financial Forecasts: 80%

4. Compliance and Audit:

○ Annual Audit Costs: AED 500,000

○ Compliance-related Penalties: AED 250,000 (average over past 3 years)

5. IT Costs:

○ Annual Maintenance of Legacy Systems: AED 2,000,000

○ IT Staff Dedicated to Financial Systems: 10 FTEs

These baseline metrics provide a snapshot of Al Shifa Hospital's financial health and operational efficiency before implementing Oracle Fusion. They serve as the foundation for our ROI analysis and will help us quantify the improvements achieved.

Quantifying the Investment

Before diving into the returns, it's important to clearly outline the total investment made in implementing Oracle Fusion Financials at Al Shifa Hospital. This includes both direct and indirect costs associated with the project.

Direct Costs

1. Software Licensing: AED 5,000,000
2. Hardware Upgrades: AED 1,500,000
3. Implementation Services: AED 3,500,000
4. Staff Training: AED 750,000
5. Data Migration: AED 500,000

Indirect Costs

1. Internal Staff Time: Estimated at AED 1,000,000 (based on hours dedicated to the project)
2. Productivity Loss During Transition: Estimated at AED 500,000

Total Investment

The total investment for the Oracle Fusion implementation at Al Shifa Hospital amounted to AED 12,750,000. This figure serves as the benchmark against which we'll measure the returns generated by the new system.

Measuring Financial Impact

Now that we've established our baseline and quantified the investment, let's examine the financial impact of Oracle Fusion on Al Shifa

Hospital's operations. We'll analyze key areas where the system has driven significant improvements.

Revenue Cycle Management

One of the most immediate and tangible benefits of Oracle Fusion has been its impact on Al Shifa's revenue cycle management. Let's compare the pre- and post-implementation metrics:

1. Average Days in Accounts Receivable (AR):

  ○ Pre-implementation: 65 days

  ○ Post-implementation: 45 days

  ○ Improvement: 31% reduction

This significant reduction in AR days has had a substantial impact on Al Shifa's cash flow. With an annual revenue of AED 500 million, this 20-day improvement translates to approximately AED 27 million in accelerated cash flow.

2. Claims Denial Rate:

  ○ Pre-implementation: 12%

  ○ Post-implementation: 7%

  ○ Improvement: 42% reduction

The improved accuracy and efficiency in claims processing have led to fewer denials, resulting in faster reimbursements and reduced administrative costs associated with appeals.

3. Clean Claims Rate:

- Pre-implementation: 75%
- Post-implementation: 92%
- Improvement: 23% increase

The higher clean claims rate has significantly reduced the time and resources spent on rework and follow-ups, allowing the billing staff to focus on more value-added activities.

Cost Management

Oracle Fusion has also had a substantial impact on Al Shifa's cost management capabilities:

1. Operating Margin:

- Pre-implementation: 3.5%
- Post-implementation: 5.2%
- Improvement: 49% increase

This improvement in operating margin is a result of both increased revenue capture and more effective cost control measures enabled by Oracle Fusion.

2. Supply Chain Costs as % of Operating Expense:

- Pre-implementation: 35%
- Post-implementation: 31%
- Improvement: 11% reduction

Better visibility into spending patterns and improved vendor management have allowed Al Shifa to optimize its supply chain costs.

3. Average Days in Accounts Payable (AP):

○ Pre-implementation: 45 days

○ Post-implementation: 52 days

○ Change: 16% increase

While this might seem counterintuitive, the increase in AP days is actually a positive change. Al Shifa has been able to negotiate better payment terms with suppliers due to improved cash flow and more accurate forecasting, allowing the hospital to hold onto cash longer without negatively impacting vendor relationships.

Financial Reporting and Analytics

The implementation of Oracle Fusion has dramatically improved Al Shifa's financial reporting capabilities:

1. Time to Close Monthly Books:

○ Pre-implementation: 15 days

○ Post-implementation: 5 days

○ Improvement: 67% reduction

This significant reduction in closing time has allowed Al Shifa's finance team to spend more time on analysis and strategic planning rather than data compilation.

2. Accuracy of Financial Forecasts:

○ Pre-implementation: 80%

○ Post-implementation: 95%

○ Improvement: 19% increase

The improved accuracy of financial forecasts has enabled better decision-making and resource allocation across the hospital.

Compliance and Audit

Oracle Fusion has also had a positive impact on Al Shifa's compliance and audit processes:

1. Annual Audit Costs:

○ Pre-implementation: AED 500,000

○ Post-implementation: AED 350,000

○ Improvement: 30% reduction

The streamlined financial processes and improved data accuracy have significantly reduced the time and effort required for annual audits.

2. Compliance-related Penalties:

○ Pre-implementation: AED 250,000 (average over past 3 years)

○ Post-implementation: AED 50,000

○ Improvement: 80% reduction

Better controls and real-time visibility into financial data have helped Al Shifa avoid compliance issues and associated penalties.

IT Costs

The implementation of Oracle Fusion has also led to significant changes in Al Shifa's IT costs:

1. Annual Maintenance of Financial Systems:

○ Pre-implementation: AED 2,000,000

○ Post-implementation: AED 1,200,000

○ Improvement: 40% reduction

While the new system requires ongoing maintenance and support, the overall costs are significantly lower than maintaining the previous legacy systems.

2. IT Staff Dedicated to Financial Systems:

○ Pre-implementation: 10 FTEs

○ Post-implementation: 6 FTEs

○ Improvement: 40% reduction

The more efficient and user-friendly Oracle Fusion system has allowed Al Shifa to reallocate IT resources to other critical areas.

Calculating the ROI

Now that we've quantified the various improvements brought about by Oracle Fusion, let's calculate the overall Return on Investment (ROI) for Al Shifa Hospital.

Tangible Benefits (Annual)

1. Improved Cash Flow: AED 27,000,000
2. Reduced Claims Denials: AED 5,000,000 (estimated based on denial rate reduction)
3. Operating Margin Improvement: AED 8,500,000 (based on revenue of AED 500 million)
4. Supply Chain Cost Reduction: AED 10,000,000
5. Audit Cost Savings: AED 150,000
6. Reduced Compliance Penalties: AED 200,000
7. IT Cost Savings: AED 800,000
8. IT Staff Reallocation: AED 1,600,000 (based on average salary of AED 400,000 per FTE)

Total Annual Tangible Benefits: AED 53,250,000

Intangible Benefits

While harder to quantify, it's important to acknowledge the intangible benefits of Oracle Fusion:

1. Improved decision-making due to better financial insights
2. Enhanced employee satisfaction and productivity
3. Better vendor relationships due to more efficient processes
4. Increased confidence from stakeholders (board members, investors) in financial management
5. Improved patient satisfaction due to more efficient billing

processes

ROI Calculation

To calculate the ROI, we'll use the following formula:

ROI = (Net Benefits / Total Investment) x 100

Net Benefits (First Year) = Total Annual Tangible Benefits - Total Investment

Net Benefits (First Year) = AED 53,250,000 - AED 12,750,000 = AED 40,500,000

ROI (First Year) = (40,500,000 / 12,750,000) x 100 = 317.6%

This impressive first-year ROI of 317.6% demonstrates the significant value that Oracle Fusion has brought to Al Shifa Hospital. It's important to note that this ROI will likely increase in subsequent years as the hospital continues to realize benefits without incurring the initial implementation costs.

Long-term Impact and Projections

While the first-year results are impressive, it's crucial to consider the long-term impact of Oracle Fusion on Al Shifa Hospital's financial health and operational efficiency.

Five-Year Projection

Let's project the benefits over a five-year period, assuming a conservative growth rate of 5% per year in tangible benefits:

Year 1: AED 53,250,000

Year 2: AED 55,912,500

Year 3: AED 58,708,125

Year 4: AED 61,643,531

Year 5: AED 64,725,708

Total Benefits over 5 years: AED 294,239,864

Subtracting the initial investment of AED 12,750,000, the net benefit over five years is AED 281,489,864.

Five-Year ROI = (281,489,864 / 12,750,000) x 100 = 2,208.5%

This projected five-year ROI of 2,208.5% underscores the transformative impact of Oracle Fusion on Al Shifa Hospital's financial operations.

Strategic Implications

Beyond the quantifiable financial benefits, the implementation of Oracle Fusion has positioned Al Shifa Hospital for long-term success in several ways:

1. Scalability: The robust Oracle Fusion platform can easily accommodate Al Shifa's growth, whether through expansion of services or potential mergers and acquisitions.
2. Adaptability: The system's flexibility allows Al Shifa to quickly adapt to changing regulatory requirements or market conditions.
3. Data-Driven Decision Making: With improved financial insights, hospital leadership can make more informed strategic decisions about resource allocation, service line expansion, and capital investments.
4. Competitive Advantage: The efficiencies gained through Oracle Fusion allow Al Shifa to offer more competitive pricing for its services while maintaining profitability.
5. Innovation Enablement: With finance staff spending less time on manual processes, there's more capacity for innovative projects that can further improve patient care and hospital operations.

Benchmarking Against Industry Standards

To provide context for Al Shifa Hospital's ROI, it's valuable to compare these results with industry benchmarks for healthcare IT implementations.

According to a recent study by the Healthcare Financial Management Association (HFMA), the average ROI for large-scale financial system implementations in hospitals is approximately 200% over five years. Al Shifa's projected five-year ROI of 2,208.5% significantly outperforms this benchmark, placing the hospital in the top tier of successful implementations.

Another industry metric to consider is the payback period - the time it takes for the benefits to recoup the initial investment. The average payback period for similar projects in healthcare is 2.5 years. Al Shifa Hospital achieved payback in less than one year, further highlighting the exceptional success of this implementation.

Lessons Learned and Best Practices

Al Shifa Hospital's successful implementation and impressive ROI can be attributed to several key factors:

1. Clear Objectives: The hospital leadership established clear, measurable objectives for the Oracle Fusion implementation from the outset.
2. Strong Executive Support: The CEO and CFO's visible commitment to the project ensured organization-wide buy-in and resource allocation.
3. Comprehensive Training: Investing in thorough staff training ensured high adoption rates and efficient use of the new system.
4. Phased Implementation: By rolling out Oracle Fusion modules in phases, Al Shifa was able to manage change effectively and realize benefits incrementally.

5. Continuous Optimization: The hospital has maintained a focus on continuously improving and optimizing their use of Oracle Fusion, rather than viewing the implementation as a one-time event.

These lessons can serve as valuable guidelines for other healthcare organizations considering similar financial system transformations.

Challenges and Areas for Improvement

While the overall ROI analysis paints a highly positive picture, it's important to acknowledge that the Oracle Fusion implementation at Al Shifa Hospital was not without its challenges. Some areas where the hospital faced difficulties and sees room for further improvement include:

1. Initial Resistance to Change: Some staff members, particularly those who had been using the legacy systems for many years, initially struggled with the transition. This highlights the importance of change management strategies in IT implementations.
2. Data Migration Complexities: The process of migrating historical financial data from legacy systems to Oracle Fusion proved more complex than initially anticipated, causing some delays in the early stages of the project.
3. Customization vs. Standardization: Balancing the desire for customized features with the benefits of using standard Oracle Fusion functionalities was an ongoing challenge. While some customizations were necessary, excessive customization can increase costs and complicate future upgrades.
4. Interoperability with Clinical Systems: While Oracle Fusion has significantly improved financial operations, there's still work to be done in fully integrating it with Al Shifa's clinical

systems to provide a complete picture of hospital performance.

5. Advanced Analytics Utilization: While the reporting capabilities of Oracle Fusion are robust, Al Shifa recognizes that they're not yet fully leveraging the advanced analytics features of the system. This represents an opportunity for future value creation.

Addressing these challenges and capitalizing on these improvement opportunities could potentially drive even greater ROI in the coming years.

Stakeholder Perspectives

The impact of Oracle Fusion extends beyond just the numbers. Let's consider the perspectives of various stakeholders at Al Shifa Hospital:

1. CFO, Fatima Al Mansouri:
"Oracle Fusion has transformed our financial operations. The real-time visibility into our financial performance has enabled us to make faster, more informed decisions. The efficiency gains have allowed our finance team to shift from being mere scorekeepers to true strategic partners in the organization."
2. CEO, Dr. Ahmed Al Hashemi:
"The implementation of Oracle Fusion has been a game-changer for Al Shifa Hospital. Not only have we seen significant financial improvements, but the enhanced data accuracy and reporting capabilities have also improved our ability to meet regulatory requirements and optimize our services for better patient care."
3. Head of IT, Zain Farooq:
"From an IT perspective, Oracle Fusion has significantly reduced the complexity of our financial systems landscape.

The cloud-based solution has improved our system reliability and reduced the burden on our IT team, allowing us to focus on more strategic initiatives."

4. Head of Billing, Laila Khalid:
   "Oracle Fusion has streamlined our billing processes dramatically. The reduction in claims denials and improved clean claims rate have not only improved our cash flow but also reduced the stress and workload on our billing staff."
5. Chief of Medical Staff, Dr. Sami Nasser:
   "While I was initially skeptical about how a financial system could impact patient care, I've been impressed by the indirect benefits. The improved financial health of the hospital has allowed for investments in new medical equipment and technologies that directly benefit our patients."

These diverse perspectives underscore the wide-ranging impact of the Oracle Fusion implementation across Al Shifa Hospital.

Future Opportunities

As Al Shifa Hospital looks to the future, several opportunities exist to further leverage Oracle Fusion and drive additional value:

1. Advanced Analytics and AI: Exploring the advanced analytics and artificial intelligence capabilities of Oracle Fusion could provide even deeper insights into financial trends and opportunities for optimization.
2. Expansion to Other Modules: Considering the success of the financial modules, Al Shifa could explore implementing other Oracle Fusion modules such as Supply Chain Management or Human Capital Management to drive further operational improvements.
3. Benchmarking and Best Practices: Utilizing Oracle Fusion's

benchmarking capabilities to compare Al Shifa's performance against industry peers could identify additional areas for improvement.

4. Predictive Modeling: Leveraging the rich data now available in Oracle Fusion to develop predictive models for patient volumes, resource needs, and financial performance could enhance strategic planning.
5. Robotic Process Automation (RPA): Integrating RPA tools with Oracle Fusion could automate even more routine tasks, further improving efficiency and reducing errors.

These opportunities suggest that while the ROI realized so far is impressive, there's potential for even greater returns in the future as Al Shifa continues to optimize its use of Oracle Fusion.

Conclusion

The implementation of Oracle Fusion Financials at Al Shifa Hospital has yielded impressive returns, both in terms of quantifiable financial benefits and broader operational improvements. The first-year ROI of 317.6% and projected five-year ROI of 2,208.5% significantly outperform industry benchmarks, positioning Al Shifa as a leader in financial management among healthcare providers.

Key improvements include enhanced revenue cycle management, more effective cost control, streamlined financial reporting, and reduced compliance risks. These benefits have not only improved the hospital's financial health but have also indirectly contributed to better patient care through enabling investments in new technologies and services.

While challenges were encountered along the way, the overall success of the implementation can be attributed to clear objectives, strong leadership support, comprehensive training, and a commitment to continuous improvement. The lessons learned from Al Shifa's experience provide valuable insights for other healthcare organizations considering similar financial transformations.

Looking ahead, Al Shifa Hospital is well-positioned to continue deriving value from its Oracle Fusion implementation. By addressing current challenges and capitalizing on future opportunities, the hospital can potentially realize even greater returns in the coming years.

Ultimately, the successful implementation of Oracle Fusion at Al Shifa Hospital demonstrates the transformative power of modern financial systems in healthcare. It underscores how strategic investments in financial technology can drive not only monetary returns but also support an organization's broader mission of providing high-quality patient care.

Chapter 20 - Lessons Learned and Future Outlook

Introduction

As we conclude our journey through Al Shifa Hospital's transformative experience with Oracle Fusion, it's time to reflect on the valuable lessons learned and consider the future prospects for the organization. This chapter will summarize the key takeaways from the implementation process, discuss the impact on the hospital's financial management, and explore how Al Shifa plans to leverage Oracle Fusion for continued success in the years to come.

Key Lessons Learned

1. The Importance of Thorough Planning

One of the most critical lessons learned during Al Shifa Hospital's Oracle Fusion implementation was the paramount importance of thorough planning. The success of the project hinged on the meticulous preparation that took place before the first line of code was written or the first module was configured.

Dr. Fatima, the hospital's CEO, reflects, "We underestimated the complexity of the planning phase initially. However, we quickly realized that investing time in comprehensive planning paid dividends throughout the implementation process."

The planning phase included:

- Detailed assessment of existing financial processes
- Identification of pain points and areas for improvement

- Clear definition of project goals and objectives
- Establishment of realistic timelines and milestones
- Allocation of resources and budget
- Risk assessment and mitigation strategies

Mr. Hassan, the CFO, adds, "Our thorough planning allowed us to anticipate potential challenges and develop contingency plans. This foresight proved invaluable when we encountered unexpected hurdles during the implementation."

2. The Value of Stakeholder Engagement

Another crucial lesson was the significance of engaging all stakeholders from the outset of the project. Al Shifa Hospital learned that successful implementation of Oracle Fusion required buy-in and active participation from various departments and levels of the organization.

Dr. Aisha, the Chief Medical Officer, shares her perspective: "Initially, some of our medical staff were skeptical about the new system. They worried it might add to their administrative burden. By involving them early in the process and addressing their concerns, we were able to turn skeptics into advocates."

The hospital implemented several strategies to ensure stakeholder engagement:

- Regular town hall meetings to update staff on project progress
- Formation of cross-functional teams to provide input on system configuration

- Appointment of department-specific "Oracle Champions" to liaison between their teams and the implementation team

- Continuous feedback loops to address concerns and incorporate suggestions

3. The Necessity of Comprehensive Training

The implementation team at Al Shifa Hospital quickly realized that the success of Oracle Fusion hinged not just on the technology itself, but on the ability of staff to effectively use the system. This led to a renewed focus on comprehensive training programs.

Mr. Ali, the Head of IT, explains, "We initially underestimated the learning curve associated with Oracle Fusion. We had to pivot quickly and develop a more robust training program to ensure all users were comfortable with the new system."

The revised training approach included:

- Role-based training modules tailored to specific job functions

- Hands-on workshops and simulation exercises

- Creation of a dedicated Oracle Fusion help desk

- Development of user-friendly manuals and quick reference guides

- Ongoing refresher courses and advanced training options

4. The Power of Data Quality

Throughout the implementation process, Al Shifa Hospital learned the critical importance of data quality. The team discovered that the effectiveness of Oracle Fusion was directly correlated to the accuracy and completeness of the data fed into the system.

Ms. Laila, the Data Migration Lead, shares her insights: "We encountered several challenges during the data migration phase due to inconsistencies and gaps in our legacy data. This experience taught us the value of maintaining high data quality standards not just for the migration, but as an ongoing practice."

Key takeaways regarding data quality included:

- The need for thorough data cleansing before migration
- Implementation of data governance policies and procedures
- Regular data audits and quality checks
- Investment in data management tools and technologies
- Cultivation of a data-driven culture across the organization

5. The Benefits of Phased Implementation

Al Shifa Hospital's decision to adopt a phased approach to implementing Oracle Fusion proved to be a wise one. This strategy allowed the team to manage the complexity of the project more effectively and provided opportunities for learning and adjustment along the way.

Dr. Fatima reflects, "The phased approach gave us the flexibility to fine-tune our implementation strategy as we progressed. It also helped maintain staff morale by delivering tangible benefits at each stage of the project."

The benefits of phased implementation included:

- Reduced risk by allowing for adjustments based on lessons learned
- Easier change management as staff could adapt gradually
- Ability to demonstrate ROI at various stages of the project
- Opportunity to build momentum and enthusiasm as each phase succeeded
- More manageable workload for the implementation team

Impact on Financial Management

The implementation of Oracle Fusion has had a profound impact on Al Shifa Hospital's financial management practices. The integrated nature of the system has brought about improvements in efficiency, accuracy, and decision-making capabilities.

Enhanced Financial Visibility

One of the most significant benefits has been the increased visibility into the hospital's financial operations. Mr. Hassan explains, "With Oracle Fusion, we now have real-time access to financial data across all departments. This transparency has revolutionized our ability to make informed decisions quickly."

The enhanced financial visibility has led to:

- More accurate financial forecasting and budgeting
- Quicker identification and resolution of financial discrepancies
- Improved cash flow management
- Better resource allocation based on up-to-date financial information

Streamlined Financial Processes

Oracle Fusion has enabled Al Shifa Hospital to streamline many of its financial processes, leading to significant time and cost savings. Automated workflows, integrated modules, and standardized procedures have eliminated many manual tasks and reduced the risk of errors.

Ms. Noura, the Accounts Payable Manager, shares her experience: "Our invoice processing time has been cut in half since implementing Oracle Fusion. The system's automated three-way matching feature has not only saved time but also improved our accuracy and reduced payment errors."

Key process improvements include:

- Automated account reconciliations
- Streamlined month-end and year-end closing processes
- Simplified compliance and audit procedures
- Integrated procurement and accounts payable processes
- Automated fixed asset tracking and depreciation calculations

Improved Financial Reporting

The robust reporting capabilities of Oracle Fusion have transformed Al Shifa Hospital's financial reporting practices. The ability to generate customized reports quickly and easily has enhanced the finance team's ability to provide meaningful insights to stakeholders.

Mr. Hassan notes, "Our board meetings are now more productive because we can present comprehensive financial reports that are both accurate and easy to understand. The visual analytics features of Oracle Fusion have been particularly well-received."

Improvements in financial reporting include:

- Real-time financial dashboards for executives
- Customizable report templates for different stakeholders
- Drill-down capabilities for detailed analysis
- Automated generation of regulatory reports
- Integration of financial and operational data for holistic reporting

Enhanced Cost Control

Oracle Fusion has provided Al Shifa Hospital with powerful tools for cost control and management. The detailed visibility into financial transactions and the ability to analyze costs at a granular level have enabled more effective cost containment strategies.

Dr. Fatima shares, "We've been able to identify and address cost overruns much more quickly. For example, we noticed an unexpected increase in supply costs in our radiology department and were able to investigate and resolve the issue within days rather than weeks."

Cost control improvements include:

- Better tracking of departmental budgets and variances
- More accurate cost allocation for services and procedures
- Improved vendor management and contract negotiations
- Enhanced ability to identify and eliminate wasteful spending
- More effective inventory management to reduce carrying costs

Leveraging Oracle Fusion for Future Success

As Al Shifa Hospital looks to the future, the team is excited about the potential to further leverage Oracle Fusion to drive continued financial success and operational excellence.

Expanding Analytical Capabilities

One of the key focus areas for the future is to expand the use of Oracle Fusion's analytical capabilities. Mr. Ali explains, "We've only scratched the surface of what's possible with the system's analytics tools. We're planning to invest in additional training and resources to fully utilize these features."

Future plans for analytics include:

- Development of predictive models for financial forecasting
- Integration of artificial intelligence for anomaly detection and fraud prevention

- Creation of more sophisticated KPI dashboards for different organizational levels

- Utilization of scenario planning tools for strategic decision-making

- Implementation of advanced cost modeling for service line profitability analysis

Enhancing Integration with Clinical Systems

While Oracle Fusion has already improved financial management at Al Shifa Hospital, there are plans to enhance its integration with clinical systems to provide an even more comprehensive view of hospital operations.

Dr. Aisha shares her vision: "By more closely integrating our financial and clinical data, we can gain deeper insights into the relationship between clinical outcomes and financial performance. This will be crucial for our value-based care initiatives."

Integration plans include:

- Linking clinical quality metrics with financial performance data

- Implementing activity-based costing for more accurate procedure pricing

- Developing a unified patient financial record that includes clinical and financial information

- Creating integrated dashboards that combine clinical and financial KPIs

- Enhancing revenue cycle management through better clinical documentation integration

Exploring Cloud Capabilities

Al Shifa Hospital is also considering a move to Oracle Fusion Cloud to take advantage of its additional features and reduced infrastructure requirements.

Mr. Ali explains the potential benefits: "Moving to the cloud could provide us with greater scalability, automatic updates, and enhanced security features. It's definitely something we're exploring as we plan for the future."

Potential advantages of moving to the cloud include:

- Reduced IT infrastructure costs
- Automatic software updates and new feature releases
- Enhanced disaster recovery and business continuity capabilities
- Improved accessibility for remote work and multi-site operations
- Easier integration with other cloud-based healthcare solutions

Continuous Process Improvement

The implementation of Oracle Fusion has instilled a culture of continuous improvement at Al Shifa Hospital. The team is committed to ongoing refinement and optimization of their financial processes.

Ms. Noura shares, "We've established a cross-functional 'Oracle Fusion Optimization Team' that meets regularly to identify areas for improvement and implement best practices."

Continuous improvement initiatives include:

- Regular review and refinement of financial workflows
- Ongoing user feedback collection and system enhancements
- Benchmarking against industry best practices
- Exploration of new Oracle Fusion features and modules
- Regular training and skill development for finance staff

Expanding to Other Hospital Functions

While the initial focus of Oracle Fusion implementation was on financial management, Al Shifa Hospital is now exploring ways to extend the system's capabilities to other areas of hospital operations.

Dr. Fatima explains, "We're looking at how Oracle Fusion can support our human resources, supply chain, and project management functions. The potential for an integrated system across all these areas is exciting."

Potential areas for expansion include:

- Implementation of Oracle Human Capital Management for improved workforce management
- Utilization of Oracle Supply Chain Management for enhanced inventory and procurement processes

- Adoption of Oracle Project Portfolio Management for better tracking of capital projects and strategic initiatives

- Exploration of Oracle Enterprise Performance Management for more sophisticated budgeting and planning

Conclusion

The implementation of Oracle Fusion at Al Shifa Hospital has been a transformative journey, marked by challenges, learnings, and significant achievements. As the hospital reflects on the lessons learned and looks to the future, it's clear that Oracle Fusion has not only revolutionized its financial management practices but has also set the stage for continued innovation and improvement across the organization.

Dr. Fatima concludes, "Oracle Fusion has given us the tools to navigate the complex financial landscape of modern healthcare. But more than that, it has instilled in us a culture of data-driven decision-making and continuous improvement. As we look to the future, we're excited about the possibilities that lie ahead."

As Al Shifa Hospital continues to leverage Oracle Fusion to its full potential, it stands as a shining example of how technology, when implemented thoughtfully and used effectively, can drive financial success and support the delivery of high-quality healthcare. The journey of Al Shifa Hospital serves as an inspiration and a roadmap for other healthcare organizations embarking on their own digital transformation journeys.

As we conclude our journey through Al Shifa Hospital's transformative experience with Oracle Fusion, it's clear that the impact of this implementation extends far beyond mere technological upgrade. The hospital's financial landscape has been fundamentally reshaped, with improved efficiency, accuracy, and insight permeating every aspect of its operations. From streamlined billing processes to enhanced vendor management, from precise asset tracking to powerful analytics, Oracle Fusion has proven to be a comprehensive solution to the complex financial challenges faced by modern healthcare institutions.

The story of Al Shifa Hospital serves as a testament to the power of embracing innovative financial management systems in the healthcare sector. It highlights the importance of careful planning, stakeholder engagement, and continuous improvement in driving successful digital transformations. The challenges faced during implementation, from data migration to user training, underscore the complexity of such projects. Yet, the hospital's ability to overcome these hurdles demonstrates the potential for positive change when leadership, staff, and technology partners work together towards a common goal.

Perhaps the most significant lesson from Al Shifa's experience is the profound impact that improved financial management can have on patient care. By optimizing its financial processes, the hospital has freed up resources and gained insights that ultimately contribute to better healthcare delivery. The integration of Oracle Fusion with other hospital systems has created a more cohesive and efficient operational environment, allowing staff to focus more on patient needs and less on administrative tasks.

As we look to the future, it's evident that the journey of financial transformation at Al Shifa Hospital is far from over. The implementation of Oracle Fusion has laid a solid foundation for ongoing improvement and innovation. The hospital's commitment to leveraging the full potential of the system promises continued gains in efficiency, compliance, and financial health. This, in turn, positions Al Shifa to better serve its community and adapt to the ever-evolving healthcare landscape.

The success story of Al Shifa Hospital offers valuable insights for other healthcare institutions considering similar transformations. It demonstrates that with the right technology, approach, and mindset, hospitals can overcome financial challenges and emerge stronger, more efficient, and better equipped to fulfill their crucial mission of providing quality healthcare. As the healthcare industry continues to face financial pressures and regulatory challenges, the example set by Al Shifa Hospital and its implementation of Oracle Fusion shines as a beacon of possibility and progress.

About the Author

Sushil Kumar is a seasoned professional with over 30 years of experience driving business value and innovation through technology, currently an Associate Vice President (AVP) in the Healthcare Industry and a Doctoral Researcher specializing in Emerging Technologies and Generative AI. His extensive background includes leading large-scale digital transformations and implementing advanced data analysis strategies across various sectors. Sushil is also a Global Professor of Practice for an U.S university, where he shares his expertise in digital transformation and business management. Beyond his professional accomplishments, Sushil embarked on a profound spiritual journey from 2005 to 2018, which deepened his commitment to living in awareness and mindfulness. He passionately advocates for integrating mindfulness into the workplace, believing it fosters greater focus, creativity, and emotional intelligence among professionals.

www.ingramcontent.com/pod-product-compliance
Lightning Source LLC
LaVergne TN
LVHW052306200926
848481LV00002B/477